Cutting and Self-Harm

CUTTING AND SELF-HARM

Chris Simpson

Health and Medical Issues Today

 GREENWOOD™

An Imprint of ABC-CLIO, LLC
Santa Barbara, California • Denver, Colorado

Library of Congress Cataloging-in-Publication Data

Simpson, Chris, 1969–
    Cutting and self-harm / Chris Simpson.
        pages cm. — (Health and medical issues today)
    Includes bibliographical references and index.
    ISBN 978–1–61069–872–6 (hardback : acid-free paper) — ISBN 978–1–61069–873–3 (ebook) 1. Cutting (Self-mutilation) 2. Self-injurious behavior. I. Title.
RC569.5.S48S56   2015
616.85'82—dc23   2015012173

ISBN: 978–1–61069–872–6
EISBN: 978–1–61069–873–3

19 18 17 16 15   1 2 3 4 5

This book is also available on the World Wide Web as an eBook.
Visit www.abc-clio.com for details.

Greenwood
An Imprint of ABC-CLIO, LLC

ABC-CLIO, LLC
130 Cremona Drive, P.O. Box 1911
Santa Barbara, California 93116-1911

This book is printed on acid-free paper ∞

Manufactured in the United States of America

CONTENTS

SERIES FOREWORD

Every day, the public is bombarded with information on developments in medicine and health care. Whether it is on the latest techniques in treatment or research, or on concerns over public health threats, this information directly affects the lives of people more than almost any other issue. Although there are many sources for understanding these topics—from Web sites and blogs to newspapers and magazines—students and ordinary citizens often need one resource that makes sense of the complex health and medical issues affecting their daily lives.

The *Health and Medical Issues Today* series provides just such a one-stop resource for obtaining a solid overview of the most controversial areas of health care in the 21st century. Each volume addresses one topic and provides a balanced summary of what is known. These volumes provide an excellent first step for students and lay people interested in understanding how health care works in our society today.

Each volume is broken into several sections to provide readers and researchers with easy access to the information they need:

Part I provides overview chapters on background information—including chapters on such areas as the historical, scientific, medical, social, and legal issues involved—that an individual needs to intelligently understand the topic.

Part II provides capsule examinations of the most heated contemporary issues and debates, and analyzes in a balanced manner the viewpoints held by various advocates in the debates.

Part III provides a selection of reference material, such as annotated primary source documents, a timeline of important events, and a directory of organizations that serve as the best next step in learning about the topic at hand.

The *Health and Medical Issues Today* series strives to provide readers with all the information needed to begin making sense of some of the most important debates going on in the world today. The series includes volumes on such topics as stem-cell research, obesity, gene therapy, alternative medicine, organ transplantation, mental health, and more.

PREFACE

I remember the first time I encountered a self-injuring client. I was a newly minted, licensed professional counselor intern working in an intensive outpatient chemical dependency program. I noticed the forearm of a client one day. He had what appeared to be small, round holes in his right forearm. I asked, "What happened to your arm?" His response was, "Sometimes I put a cigarette out in my arm. It sort of snaps me out of it." At the time, I was not sure what "it" would have been. In fact, I genuinely did not conceive self-injurious behavior. From that point, I began to notice the behavior in other clients, and my quest for understanding began.

I realized that, while confusing to most of us, self-injury actually serves a very real purpose for the individual employing the behavior. The purpose of this book is to clarify the motivations for the behavior and highlight the components that surround self-injury. Part I of the book is concerned with defining the behavior and identifying its origins. Chapter 1 provides definitions to important terms. Additionally, history of the behavior and basic characteristics are addressed. Chapter 2 addresses factors that contribute to self-injury, including biological and environmental factors. Chapter 3 addresses conditions that frequently exist in conjunction with self-injury. Chapter 4 discusses how to address self-injury from a variety of different roles. Chapter 5 describes the process of treatment of self-injury.

Part II was designed to address controversial issues that surround self-injury. Chapter 6 addresses self-injury in school settings. This is perhaps the most controversial setting for this issue. School settings seem to experience self-injurers in significant numbers. Overall, school professionals find this behavior distressing and confusing. Chapter 7 addresses how self-injury can affect relationships. Chapter 8 addresses group counseling and its relationship and potential effectiveness in treating self-injury. And finally, Chapter 9 addresses the use of psychopharmacology in treating self-injury. Part III of the book provides a variety of resources including related books, websites, and articles. Some important documents are included, as well as a glossary, timeline, and bibliography.

This book was designed to address the most topical and relevant issues surrounding the behavior of self-injury. Hopefully, parents, friends, mental health professionals, and those who practice self-injury can find this book useful.

ACKNOWLEDGMENTS

To begin, I would like to thank my friends at ABC-CLIO. Your faith in my ability to write this manuscript is greatly appreciated.

To my colleagues who granted interviews, support, and endless phone calls, I thank you for your patience and willingness.

To my mother, Delpha, thanks for being my encouraging voice. Just like a mom, you were always willing to offer words of encouragement.

To my dad, Jeff, thanks for sharing in the pride and joy of completing this manuscript. It means more than you know.

And, finally, to my wife, Kristin, thank you for your endless encouragement and understanding through this process and so many others. Your love and grace mean so much. You are the greatest partner I could ever hope for. I love you very much.

PART I

Cutting and Self-Harm: What Are They and How Do They Occur?

CHAPTER 1

Cutting and Self-Harm: Definitions, History, and Basic Characteristics

Cutting and self-harm have served as confusing and troubling behaviors in North American and European cultures especially since the late twentieth century. The amount of literature, nonfiction and fiction alike, on the subject has increased substantially since the early 1980s. Self-harm has worked its way into popular culture through movies, books, and electronic media. More reports of self-harming behaviors have emerged in schools and clinical settings like treatment facilities and hospitals. Self-harm has developed into a very tangible and, for many, terrifying behavior that demands the attention of communities and helping professionals alike. As the world has become more informed of the potential dangers of this behavior, self-harm has become more globally recognized as a health threat to those who commit such acts.

While there is a great deal of evidence that would suggest cutting and self-harm have existed for hundreds or even thousands of years, modern society has difficulty tolerating the existence of this phenomenon. Mental health professionals, parents, teachers, friends, and caregivers often find themselves in distress when faced with the prospect of managing or even confronting a loved one who commits self-harm. This distress has manifested itself honestly as stopping self-injurious behavior can be both difficult and painful for all involved.

It would appear that the solution to self-harming behaviors is simple. If the individual will stop cutting or self-injuring, then all related problems will cease. Of course, the concept of ceasing self-harming behavior for the individual or those close to that individual is not so simple. In fact, there is much to understand about self-harm before making any determinations about how to move forward. Perhaps the best way toward a better understanding of self-harm is defining the variety of terms often related to the behavior. Self-harm has been considered appropriate in some environments and cultures. The chapter will provide some understanding of this. Additionally, the prevalence of self-harm will be discussed.

DEFINITIONS AND IMPORTANT TERMINOLOGY
Self-Harm

There are many terms that can assist in better understanding self-harm. To begin, the term "self-harm" should be defined. Self-harm can include many different behaviors that fit under one umbrella. Self-harm may be seen as a spectrum of behaviors that can result in harm to the individual. In summary, those behaviors that may be seen as self-harming may include (but not be limited to) alcohol or substance abuse, eating disorders, and, of course, cutting, burning, or scarring.

By this definition, an individual could consume a substance (e.g., alcohol, nicotine, marijuana, cocaine, heroin, hydrocodone, and so on) to the point of damaging vital organs like the heart, lungs, liver, or kidneys. The concept of self-harm could be taken a step further in that an intoxicated individual could operate a vehicle under the influence resulting in a wreck. The outcome could be injury or even death. Certainly, this is self-harming as the individual knowingly consumed the substance to achieve intoxication.

Another individual could suffer from anorexia nervosa. This is a condition in which the individual will withhold food or exercise obsessively in order to maintain a certain body weight. This individual may subject him- or herself to excessive calorie restriction or withhold food altogether with the purpose of maintaining a perceived ideal weight or body image.

Another individual may suffer from bulimia nervosa. In this case, the person may binge on food and then purge it through vomiting, through the use of diuretics, or through laxatives in order to maintain a certain weight or body image. In either case, it is important to note that a distorted body image is in place and self-harm will most certainly be the result. Much like anorexia, the damage may be in the form of damaged tissue. Any of the previous three examples could be viewed as self-harming. All of these behaviors can result in damage to the body. However, these behaviors do not specifically describe deliberately damaging the skin through cutting, burning, or scarring. This hastens the next definition of self-injury.

Self-Injury

Self-injury has a much more specific definition than self-harm. There are several variations on the definition. However, the literature appears to agree that self-injury is defined as the deliberate destruction of one's own bodily tissue with the intent of avoiding emotions that are considered intolerable by the individual. By inflicting a wound to the skin, the individual does not have to experience aversive emotional experiences. In short, an individual who participates in self-injury by cutting, burning, or otherwise damaging the skin is attempting to avoid feelings of pain, anxiety, shame, or anger, among other emotions. Karen Conterio and Wendy Lader (1998) provide an extensive list of acts that can be considered self-injury including:

- cutting
- hitting oneself
- extracting hair to excess
- head banging
- scratching to excess
- biting oneself
- burning oneself
- interfering with the healing of wounds
- breaking bones
- chewing the lip, tongue, or fingers
- eye enucleation (removal)
- amputation of limbs, breasts, digits, or genitals
- facial skinning
- ingesting sharp or toxic objects

This list provides a variety of self-injurious behaviors that require expanded definitions provided in the pages to follow.

With increased attention toward this behavior through research and popular media alike, several variations on the definition of self-injury exist. Most of these definitions have included all of the components previously mentioned. However, over the years, much attention has been given to the intent of self-injury. Specifically, the question of suicidal ideation has been attached to the behavior. A lack of clarity has existed for those unfamiliar with the behavior. For many, it would be easy to identify self-injury as an attempt at suicide as opposed to the self-regulating behavior that it is. This spawned the need for a more specific definition.

Nonsuicidal Self-Injury

The most recent definition of self-injury is the deliberate destruction of one's own bodily tissue with the intent of avoiding emotions that are considered intolerable by the individual without the intent to commit suicide. The new component to this definition is *without the intent to commit suicide*. This more complete definition of self-injury, referred to almost exclusively as nonsuicidal self-injury (NSSI), better classifies the behavior. It is now clear that NSSI is a separate and distinct issue from suicidal behavior.

In the fifth edition of the *Diagnostic and Statistical Manual of Mental Disorders* (DSM-5), released in 2013, NSSI now possesses its own diagnosis. This is different from the *Diagnostic and Statistical Manual of Mental Disorders, Fourth Edition, Text Revision* (DSM-IV-TR, 2000), which identified NSSI as one of the diagnostic criteria for borderline personality disorder, as well as factitious disorders. Borderline personality disorder and factitious disorders can now be found in Section II of the DSM-5 under "Personality Disorders" and "Somatic Symptoms and Related Disorders," respectively, while NSSI can be found in the third section of the DSM-5, entitled "Emerging Measures and Models."

Suicide

Suicide may be defined as the act of killing oneself intentionally. When an individual is thinking about committing suicide, that individual is participating in suicidal ideation. In most countries around the world, a suicide threat is taken very seriously. A great deal of research has been conducted on suicide, yielding a variety of statistics, risk factors, and treatment. Many organizations, including, but not limited to, the American Foundation for Suicide Prevention, the American Association of Suicidology, the Jed Foundation, and the National Alliance on Mental Illness, have been formed to improve efforts to prevent and treat suicide. Certainly, a link between self-harm and suicide exists. In fact, many experts would agree that attempted suicide is a form of what will later be described as indirect self-harm.

The arguments for and against suicide are many and deserving of extensive debate. Those discussions are beyond the scope of this particular text. However, a few points on the topic should be noted. To begin, in most Western societies, suicide is not punishable by law, while in some countries like India and North Korea, attempted suicide can be accompanied by legal ramifications like a fine and up to one year in prison. In the United States, suicide has been historically viewed as an illegal act. However, into the late 1980s, less than half of the states possessed laws against attempting suicide or even completing the act. By the early 1990s, only two states still identified suicide as a crime.

Laws do exist in every state declaring it a felony to assist or encourage another person to commit suicide. Euthanasia, defined as intentionally terminating a life to end pain and suffering, is currently one of the most researched topics in the field of bioethics. This is a highly debated topic across the world, and many different opinions and concerns exist on the subject.

In the United States, physician-assisted suicide has become legal in four states to date (at the time of this publication those states are Montana, Vermont, Washington State, and Oregon). There appear to be some common variables that must be present for physician-assisted suicide to be legal. First, the individual in question must be a legal resident of the state in which physician-assisted suicide may be administered. Second, a physician and a consulting physician must determine that the individual suffers from an incurable, terminal illness. Third, the individual must express a desire to die. And, last, the individual must self-administer the lethal agent, in this case usually a medication that will hasten death.

In terms of its relationship to self-harm, obviously suicide would qualify as a self-harming behavior. However, it is important to note that the existence of self-injury does not necessarily mean that suicidal ideation is present. Anecdotally, some who participate in self-injury have identified the behavior as helpful in avoiding suicidal thoughts. This progression in thought would suggest that self-injury, while maladaptive, can serve as a coping behavior.

Trichotillomania

Trichotillomania is the compulsive urge to pull one's hair out of the skin. Common areas from which one may remove the hair are the scalp, eyelashes, eyebrows, pubic area, arms, legs, hands, and nose. In the DSM-5, trichotillomania is identified as an obsessive-compulsive disorder. An important distinction between trichotillomania and nonsuicidal self-injury is this difference in diagnosis as nonsuicidal self-injury is not seen as an obsessive-compulsive disorder.

For example, if trichotillomania is a compulsion, this suggests that an irresistible urge exists to pull the hair from the skin. One might pull the hair without a thought about it or unconsciously. No distinction will be made that the individual is removing his or her hair in front of others at a perceived appropriate time or alone in one's bedroom. The compulsion is irresistible and committed with no regard for place or time. Nonsuicidal self-injury typically begins with a buildup of emotion, irritability, or anxiety that is relieved when the self-injury occurs. Consequently, nonsuicidal self-injury may be considered more of an impulsive behavior often accompanied by rituals that are frequently, if not always, performed around the behavior. For example, many people who practice self-injury may attempt to self-injure at the same time of day or with the same instrument. However, while certain repetitive behaviors may occur along with self-harm, most report an ability to commit the act at a time of their choosing. Clearly, trichotillomania may be seen as a self-harming behavior. However, it possesses very distinct differences from nonsuicidal self-injury.

Excoriation

Excoriation, like trichotillomania, is considered an obsessive-compulsive disorder and may be found in the DSM-5 under "Obsessive-Compulsive and Related Disorders." Excoriation, or to use the clinical terminology, excoriation disorder, refers to picking the skin. An individual who participates in this behavior will obsessively pick at the skin until a lesion or scarring may appear. Frequently, excoriation begins with a wound that has formed a scab or perhaps some minor skin imperfection like a mole or blemish. The individual will then pick at the wound or imperfection compulsively. Like trichotillomania, there is an irresistible quality about the behavior. The individual will pick with little to no regard for surroundings or environment. Consequently, wounds or skin imperfections that were otherwise easily remedied may become infected, deeper and more severe, and even scarred.

Direct versus Indirect Self-Harm

With the recent shift in definition from self-injury to nonsuicidal self-injury, a previously established pair of terms has reemerged. These terms are "direct self-harm" and "indirect self-harm." Direct self-harm is another term for intentionally cutting, burning, or mutilating the skin for the purpose of regulating emotions. With direct self-harm, the damage is immediate and intentional. In other words, the individual participating in direct self-harm is triggered (e.g., feels anxiety or a sense of uneasiness) and inflicts a wound on the body with an instrument of choice.

Indirect self-harm is a more ambiguous prospect. This form of self-harm can appear in many forms. Damage from indirect self-harm is cumulative and usually delayed. In the case of alcohol abuse, an adolescent who consumes excessive amounts of alcohol will not reap the biological and psychological effects immediately unless, of course, the individual is in some sort of disabling or even fatal accident. Assuming the individual avoids such an event, the effects may be seen years later after repetitive abuse of the substance.

Indirect self-harm is not limited to alcohol and substance abuse or addiction. Eating disorders like anorexia nervosa, bulimia nervosa, and compulsive overeating would align under the classification of indirect self-harm. Smoking, texting while operating machinery, withholding necessary medications, and risk-taking behavior are all forms of indirect self-harm.

Body Modification

Body modification has been the source of some debate in regard to its relationship with self-injurious behavior. Body modification can be described as deliberately altering one's anatomy through piercing, tattooing, branding, or scarification. Body modification is often employed for aesthetic reasons. Put simply, the individual appreciates the appearance of the modification. Body modification can also facilitate a rite of passage or display a religious belief. There are many examples of body art, branding, or scarring showing the individual's association to a particular group like a fraternity, gang, or team. In some instances, piercings to the penis or labia have been reported to increase sexual stimulation. Many reasons exist for committing body modification. The prevailing question is whether body modification should be considered a form of self-injury.

Examples of body piercing and tattooing have been scattered throughout history for thousands of years. Since the early 1990s, there has been a noticeable increase in the prevalence of piercing and tattoos in common culture. There has become a new appreciation for the art of tattooing and piercing, which has given rise to the term "body art." Brilliant displays of ink in various degrees of color and richness may be found on the skin of men and women alike. Some would even claim being "addicted to ink." More than likely, this is not an addiction but a fascination with the process or meaning of the images displayed on the skin or simply what the body art might communicate. In some circles, body modification has become as much a form of fashion as clothing or jewelry. Simply stated, body modification or body art makes a statement about the individual who adorns it.

But is body modification truly self-injurious? There is no question that blood is drawn in the process of piercing or tattooing. However, as long as appropriate safety procedures are in place, there is little danger of actual harm to the individual. Some may ask, "What if someone has multiple tattoos or piercings? Wouldn't that be self-injurious?" The answer to this question is not about number but intent.

For example, Cara has multiple piercings on her body. The crests of both ears are pierced with at least 20 hoops. Her bottom lip is pierced with six different rings. She has pierced both nostrils and nipples, and she reportedly pierced her clitoris. When asked by a friend about her new dermal anchor piercing in her chest, she proclaims, "Yeah. It really hurt. But doesn't it look fantastic!?!" In this example, Cara is concerned with the means to an end. She is interested in how the piercing looks. She tolerates, but does not seek, the pain that accompanies the piercing.

In another case, Craig has many tattoos (and several piercings). His piercings consist of multiple hoops on his ears, a dermal anchor piercing on each side of his chest, a ring in each nostril, a ring in his right eyebrow, and rings on his nipples. He also has many tattoos. He is particularly fond of the portrait of Crazy Horse that he has recently inked on his shoulder. The rich black ink with contours and textures of the face of the iconic Native American is beautifully emblazoned across Craig's front, medial, and posterior deltoid. Craig has many other tattoos, most of which are not as brilliant a display of artistry but tell a story nonetheless. He has three very simple, one-inch crosses that run in a straight line from elbow to wrist down his left interior forearm. Each cross represents the memory of his mother and two younger sisters who died in a car accident when Craig was 18 years old. These stories of body art describe different aspects of Craig. The profile of Crazy Horse represents internal beliefs Craig has about the atrocities committed to the Native American tribes in the United States. The crosses on his forearm are of a totally different intent. Craig is paying memory to loved ones lost to him. In either case, these tattoos are an expression of what is important and worth remembering to Craig. While imperative to Craig's story, these examples of body art are not terribly different from the stories of many who choose to use their skin as a canvas for self-expression. Tattoos and piercings may simply be seen as a form of self-expression. As mentioned previously, some may see these as devices of fashion. However, in these examples, it would be difficult to describe this medium as maladaptive or truly harmful to the individual.

However, if Craig were to be asked about his multiple piercings around the ears, another perspective may be gained. As Craig gently tugged on each ring while he describes it, he tells about an emotional event that can be associated with each ring and the pain that was sought when the piercing was administered. "This one is when my Mom and my sisters died. This one is when my first girlfriend left me. I really loved her. This one is when my Dad told me not to ever come back home. He and I had some disagreements you might say." The descriptions go on for each of the approximately 20 rings that are on each ear. When asked to describe what he was seeking when he received the piercings, he described that the pain of the piercing felt better than the state of being prior to the piercing. Craig had found a way to avoid internal pain by seeking physical pain through piercing. This is an example of piercing (or in other cases, tattooing) serving as a self-harming behavior. It is self-harming in that Craig is avoiding feelings of internal struggle by piercing his body. Conversely, it would be hard to describe the tattoos that Craig possesses as self-harming behavior. His tattoos serve a more conventional purpose of self-expression. Can tattoos and piercings be seen as self-harm and self-injury? Objectively, the answer would often be no. However, if probing questions find that the individual is using this medium to avoid affect, self-injury may be indicated.

Stereotypic Movement Disorder

Stereotypic movement disorder is found in the DSM-5 under "Motor Disorders" in the category of "Neurodevelopmental Disorders." The onset of this disorder is in infancy or early childhood. The behavior involves repetitive, nonfunctional movement like hand waving, head banging, rocking, and other rhythmic movements that interfere with normal functioning. Diagnosed early and treated pharmacologically, this disorder can be managed. Untreated, the disorder can yield some severe effects including brain trauma and permanent damage to other parts of the body. Other conditions exist which may be characterized by repetitive movement, including autism spectrum disorder, obsessive-compulsive disorder, and tic disorders like Tourette's syndrome.

While stereotypic movement disorder is certainly characterized as a form of self-injury, this behavior does not relate to what will be described in the following section as moderate self-injury. The term that must be considered when differentiating the two behaviors is "intent." Nonsuicidal self-injury is intentional and has a specific purpose.

Moderate versus Major Self-Injury

With the exception of stereotypic movement disorder and suicide, the definitions previously provided would be described as moderate self-injury. Those who participate in moderate self-injury are often high-functioning individuals who have found a means of coping with emotional dysregulation. For the most part, a person committing nonsuicidal self-injury or moderate self-injury knows exactly how far to cut, burn, or otherwise damage the skin in order to get the desired effect. This effect is of course escape from intolerable affect or emotion. Cases of nicked tendons or arterial tissue are sometimes a danger. But this is rare for the most part; the person committing nonsuicidal or moderate self-injury has no desire to critically wound him- or herself. The end result is usually on a spectrum of mild cuts or wounds that can easily heal (with the appropriate dressing and time) to severe scarring that may be more permanent. While scarring can be cosmetically distressing, it would not be characterized as major self-injury.

According to Armando Favazza (2011), author of the seminal text on self-injury, *Bodies under Siege: Self-Mutilation, Nonsuicidal Self-Injury, and Body Modification in Culture and Psychiatry,* major self-injury is the act of intentionally destroying significant body tissue. Examples of this kind of tissue damage would be eye enucleation (or removal), castration, or removal of a limb or digit. Barent W. Walsh (2012) states that major self-injury would meet the definition of "self-mutilation" as the individual is attempting to significantly alter or mutilate a part of the body. In fact, in clinical environments, it is commonly accepted that "major self-injury" and "self-mutilation" are terms that may be used interchangeably.

Little quantitative research on the subject of major self-injury exists. Most research completed on this topic is in the form of individual cases. With this clarifier, cases in which major self-injury has been employed involve acute distress, intoxication, or psychosis. The individual is trying to solve a problem or reportedly receiving instructions from a deity, individual, or authority figure (e.g., God or the devil). Robert Grossman (2001) notes four different types of major self-injury that may be found in the literature: genital, which involves transection of the penis, castration, or vaginal lacerations; ocular, which includes removal, puncture, or laceration; amputation of a limb or removal of a digit of the finger or toe; and rare occurrences like laceration to or attempted removal of the nose or parts of the face.

It is important to note that major self-injury is not found in typical environments related to moderate self-injury like schools, universities, and counseling offices where the individual is capable of high function. Major self-injury will most likely be found within inpatient facilities, psychiatric hospitals, or correctional facilities. While there is a great distinction that can be made between moderate and major self-injury, one quality remains consistent between these two behaviors. Both moderate and major self-injury are not attempts at suicide, respectively, but attempts at either emotional regulation or problem solving.

HISTORY OF SELF-INJURY
Religion and Self-Injury

Self-injury is not a new phenomenon, although, as previously mentioned, it has garnered a great deal of attention since the late 1980s.

In fact, while it is difficult to understand the motivation for it in North American and European culture, self-injury can be found in a variety of settings throughout cultures and history. Furthermore, there are many environments in which self-injury may be considered appropriate or even encouraged. To begin, self-injury is endorsed in some religious communities.

Flagellation is the process of whipping the human body by using instruments like a whip, a scourge, or a cat-o'-nine-tails. The practice has been endorsed among Christian and Islamic communities alike. In Christianity, the practice of self-flagellation has been present throughout the history of the religion, especially in Catholic monasteries and convents. This was a Roman practice prior to Christianity. Those under Roman rule were subjected to flagellation for the purpose of maintaining authority and demonstrating dominance. The first Christian communities adopted the Roman legal system and consequently kept flagellation in place as a means of punishment. In medieval monasteries, flagellation was used to promote obedience among the population of monks and nuns. Public displays of flogging in front of fellow monks served the purpose of subjugation to the law and also paved the way for Christian virtue.

Self-flagellation among monks refers to the flogging of Christ prior to the crucifixion. It serves as a form of repentance and purification and a means of communicating with God. Beginning in the eleventh century, self-flagellation became an appreciated act signifying a devotion to Christ and expressing human guilt, as well as preempting punishment in the afterlife. Even today, self-flagellation is promoted as a Lenten ritual. Catholic cultures throughout the United States, Mexico, the Philippines, and parts of Mediterranean Europe tolerate and even promote self-flagellation.

Among Shia Muslims, self-flagellation serves as part of the glorification and mourning ritual over the betrayal of Imam Husayn, grandson of Muhammad. In 680 CE, Husayn was betrayed by proclaimed supporters, and his attempt at a coup failed. On the 10th of Muharram, Husayn's camp was invaded and he and all of his followers were slaughtered. In the Shiite world, the tragedy of Karbala is remembered as a traumatic event and has become a key part of Shiite identity. On the 10th day of Muharram, part of this ritual includes wearing black clothes and fasting. People will intensely cry, and men will be seen violently beating their chests, self-flagellating their backs with chains, or cutting their foreheads with knives. In contrast to the Christian practice of self-flagellation, the Shiite practice is not intended to induce pain for the purpose of showing obedience or the guilt of being human but instead to show identification with the martyrs of Karbala through bleeding.

Other accounts of religiously oriented self-injury may be found around the world. In Benin, West Africa, high priests may go into a trancelike state and cut themselves signifying that a deity has entered the body. During the Qing Dynasty in the 1840s, multiple accounts of Chinese relatives offering their flesh to Heaven in exchange for saving the life of their dying loved one can be found. The process would include the individual cutting and therefore removing a part of the flesh, in most cases, the thigh. Mystical Islamic healers in Morocco will thrust themselves about in a frenzied twirling motion until achieving a level of dizziness. Then the healer will lacerate his scalp, letting blood spill. Sick and injured observers will then dip bread into the spilled blood and be healed by the ritual. In Australian aboriginal cultures, accounts exist of shaman tearing away at the flesh as an exchange for being given vision to help an ailing fellow. In some African tribes, a digit may be removed at the funeral of a loved one. The amount of the finger that is removed signifies the closeness to the deceased. In all of these examples of self-harm in the name of religion, the individuals who commit these acts do so with collectivist intentions. In other words, these acts are done not for the individual but to connect with a deity, to show caring for others in their respective communities, or to pay honor.

Self-Injury as a Rite of Passage

In some cultures, self-injury can serve as a rite of passage. In the Gahuka-Gana tribe in Papua, New Guinea, boys become initiated into adulthood by enduring the ritual of inserting sticks into the nose to induce bleeding. This is believed to promote cleansing and move the young man into adult life. Among the Satere-Mawe tribe in the Brazilian Amazon, for a boy to become a man, he must stick his hand in a glove containing bullet ants. To achieve manhood, he must endure the bites of the ants for 10 minutes without wincing or making a sound.

Many rituals exist among Northern Native Americans. For a young male in the Mandan tribe to become a man, he must first be suspended by hooks inserted into the muscles of the chest, shoulders, and back without making any noise. After losing consciousness due to blood loss and sheer pain, the young man is revived only to willingly place a finger on a block to be sacrificed to the gods. There exist countless other examples of culturally accepted self-injury for the sake of achieving a certain status in the community. While each of these examples involves enduring a self-harming act, the person is surrounded by members of the community in support of making it through the ritual. These acts are not done in secrecy or strictly in solitude. The entire community is aware of the act and, more often than not, in support of it.

Conventional Self-Injury

Self-harming behaviors like nonsuicidal self-injury tend to intimidate those who do not participate in it. For many, it is hard to imagine why someone would intentionally harm themselves without the intention of suicide. Of course, people commit self-harming acts (e.g., excessive drinking, texting while driving, and so on) regularly without considering the similarity to conventional self-injury. Conventional self-injury does not have a place in mainstream Western culture. Someone who commits conventional self-injury, also defined as nonsuicidal self-injury, is often viewed as significantly impaired in some way. As previously discussed, this is not necessarily the case. For the most part, committing a self-injurious act is a contained, isolated incident that does not limit the individual in performing daily tasks like going to work, shopping, picking up children from school, or going to a ball game. We likely do not know that the individual is self-injuring. This is often a private act of self-regulation. In a way, that is where conventional self-injury differs from culturally sanctioned self-injury as previously described.

Examples of culturally appropriate self-injury describe the individual being surrounded by those who are of a like mind. It is an act of devotion or piety. It may be intended to connect one to a deity or perhaps assist in the healing of another. In these cases, self-injury serves a purpose outside of oneself or for the benefit of the greater good or the group. Conventional self-injury is a self-contained act that does not necessarily serve the greater good (although the self-injurers might feel they are better prepared to serve after committing the act). Conventional self-injury is an act of self-maintenance that is not clearly understood by Western culture. Clearly, there is dysfunction in self-injury for the purpose of emotional regulation. However, that individual seeks the same objectives as most of society: comfort, emotional regulation, sometimes escape, and sometimes punishment.

BASIC CHARACTERISTICS

While some truly groundbreaking texts and studies exist on the subject of self-injury, researching the prevalence and basic demographics on self-injury has proven to be a challenge. Most studies on this topic have been conducted in treatment facilities, psychiatric hospitals, correctional facilities, or other environments in which it is convenient to gather such information. Few findings have yielded quantitative data revealing the prevalence of this behavior among otherwise high-functioning individuals.

This difficulty in data collection among the general population makes sense. Most people who commit nonsuicidal self-injury on a consistent basis hope to continue the behavior. Consequently, if the self-injuring individuals were to reveal themselves, someone might attempt to take that behavior away.

Whitlock et al. (2011) have completed one of the larger self-injury studies on a randomly selected sample to date. Data were gathered from eight different colleges in the northeast and midwest United States. This study provided the opportunity to study self-injury across a variety of demographics. As self-injury is no longer an overlooked public health issue, the frequency of studies has increased.

Age and Self-Injury

By most accounts in the literature, the onset or average age at which one begins to use self-injury is approximately 15 years of age. In some studies, an age range of 12–24 has been reported. In a study by Ross and Heath (2002), 59 percent of adolescents reported starting to self-injure in the seventh or eighth grade. The majority of the literature seems to agree that nonsuicidal self-injury seems to begin between adolescence and young adulthood. However, outliers do exist. Troubling reports of middle-school-aged children committing self-injury have surfaced, as well as children as young as seven. Another outlier is the prevalence of nonsuicidal self-injury among the elderly. Fewer incidents of self-injury are reported among this population, but rates appear to be increasing, particularly among older men. In contrast to adolescents and young adults, self-injury among the elderly appears to be a strong indicator for suicide. Some indicators as to why this appears to be the case may be found in the following account.

George, a 78-year-old male, had been married to his wife, Sarah, for 52 years. Approximately six months after Sarah's death by heart attack, George reported increased feelings of hopelessness. Reportedly by accident, he found some relief from feelings of anxiety and hopelessness by making a small incision in the end of his finger with his pocket knife. However, while George did report some comfort in self-injuring, he also reported a decreased desire to live without his wife. This is only one account of self-injury among this population. Contrasting examples and conclusions may be presented.

Gender and Self-Injury

Self-injury has been considered a coping practice dominated by females with male counterparts lagging far behind. The most current research confirms this to be the case. Whitlock et al. (2011) have discovered some interesting additions to these findings. In this study, which included responses from more than 11,000 college-age students (most studies in self-injury vary from participants numbering 1 to 1,000), females were more likely to report self-injurious behavior than males in lifetime prevalence of the behavior. However, males and females were equally likely to report self-injury committed in the past year. Some researchers have proposed that the prevalence of males who commit self-injury has been underestimated. In fact, some studies indicate that the disproportion of self-injury among females and males has leveled off substantially.

In addition to prevalence rates, other compelling factors are present when discussing gender and self-injury. Females reportedly tend to cut or scratch when committing self-injury and are much more prone to attend to wound care. Females also tend to report incidences of sexual abuse more often than their male counterparts. Conversely, males tend to employ self-injurious methods like burning or self-hitting. They also tend to worry less about wound care and the appearance of scars.

Whitlock et al. produced some interesting conclusions in regard to self-injury and sexual orientation. Overall, nonheterosexual individuals reported significantly higher rates of self-injury. Furthermore, mostly heterosexual males were roughly twice as likely to report nonsuicidal self-injury as exclusively heterosexual males. Women in all sexual orientation categories were more likely to report self-injury than men. A dearth of research has been completed in the relationship between nonsuicidal self-injury and sexual orientation. More inquiry would seem to be indicated and would greatly contribute to the collective body of knowledge.

Socioeconomic Status and Self-Injury

The current literature indicates that the majority of those who employ self-injury are Caucasian, female, and originating from middle to high socioeconomic status. However, an early study on self-injury by Jarvis, Ferrence, Whitehead, and Johnson (1982) found that living arrangements such as high density of housing (consistent with housing in inner cities) and single-person households were related to inflated levels of self-injury. More recently, in a study by Young, van Beinum, Sweeting, and

West, young people who reported being unemployed or sick were more likely to use self-injury as a coping mechanism. This group also reported that self-injury was not a temporary or onetime behavior but a chronic problem, suggesting that self-injury had become a consistent self-regulatory activity.

As previously mentioned, much of the research in self-injury has been conducted in psychiatric hospitals and treatment facilities. This would suggest that most research participants in this area are predominantly from middle- to upper-class socioeconomic status. Even with insurance coverage, out-of-pocket expenses for such facilities can be exceedingly expensive. Consequently, most people who can afford treatment are more often than not those who tend to be the subjects of research on self-injury. This is concerning and suggests that a bias exists in a majority of the research. Fortunately, researchers have made note of this, and more studies are being conducted among the general population. This should provide a clearer picture of demographics.

Culture and Self-Injury

When describing rates of self-injury among different cultures, a definition of culture would assist in the process. One definition of culture regards the beliefs or customs of a particular society or group. Self-injury appears to be present in a variety of groups. For example, self-injury rates ranged from 4 percent in young military recruits up to 38 percent in college-age students (Gratz, Conrad, & Roemer, 2002; Klonsky, Oltmanns, & Turkheimer, 2003). Culture can also be defined as a way of thinking or behaving that exists in a certain environment. By this definition, those who participate in self-injury could be defined as their own culture. In fact, with self-injury rates on the rise, the culture of self-injury seems to be alive and thriving. Particularly in schools (grade school and universities alike), inpatient facilities, and detention centers, self-injury is observed and, at times, promoted among peers. An alarming number of individuals (particularly adolescent and young adults) report observing self-injury among friends, associates, or classmates. This could explain why many report trying self-injury only once or maybe less than six times. This would suggest that many people who have tried self-injury have tried it at least once, and maybe it did not serve any purpose for them. For others, the experiment of self-injury is successful and employed on a regular basis.

In terms of ethnicity and self-injury, early studies suggested that self-injury is practiced primarily among Caucasian youth. In recent studies, as the breadth of populations studied has increased, numbers have varied. For example, in one study by Lloyd-Richardson, Perrine, Dierker, and Kelley (2007), of the 633 adolescents who completed the survey, approximately half (50.9%) were African American. Other studies indicate that self-injury may be more common among Caucasians while others show equally high rates among other ethnic groups. Regional variation must be considered when studying self-injury and race and ethnicity. The important factor is that self-injury and self-harming behaviors appear to be at least somewhat generalizable to the overall population. The behavior simply does not appear to settle with one particular group based on any cultural factors.

Rates of Self-Injury

In the early 1980s, Pattison and Kahan (1983) reported an estimate of 400 out of 100,000 individuals committed self-injury. In 1988, Favazza and Conterio estimated that self-injury occurred in about 750 out of 100,000 cases. By the late 1990s, estimates grew to 1,000 in 100,000. By 2005, around 2 million Americans reported participating in at least one act of self-injury (Walsh, 2012). Van Camp, Desmet, and Verhaeghe (2011) estimate about 4 percent of the general adult population in Western countries participate in nonsuicidal self-injury. As more studies are conducted on this phenomenon, it appears that self-injury is a growing behavior among a variety of ages, cultures, and ethnicities.

CONCLUSION

In conclusion, understanding the variety of terms associated with self-harm is vital if one is to possess a fully informed perspective on the behavior. Misunderstanding about self-harm is prevalent, promoting fear, frustration, and, at times, hopelessness for self-injuring individuals, their families, and helping professionals alike. By fully grasping the definition of self-harm in general, as well as its variety in manifestations and its prevalence, people can make better decisions about how to proceed with ceasing, or at least managing, the behavior. Information gained in this chapter will be applicable to the chapters that follow. Without an understanding of what self-harm is and, maybe as important, is not, approaches to this behavior appear more daunting.

CHAPTER 2

Factors Contributing to Self-Injury

A commonly asked question about self-injury is, "Why?" The concept of purposefully harming oneself is genuinely inconceivable for most. Consequently, some sort of tangible reason or cause is sought by those close to the self-injurer. Much like a switch on some sort of machine being toggled or looking under the hood of a car for a broken gasket or belt, it is only natural to point at something and proclaim, "That is the problem!" Unfortunately, it is usually not that simple. As indicated by the name of the chapter, factors contributing to the behavior must be investigated. When that investigation is complete, then a conceptualization can be made. It is rare that one's behavior can be explained by only one of these factors. More likely, a combination of factors must be considered.

The following excerpt from the Columbia Pictures film *28 Days* (2000) provides some interesting insight into self-injury. Gwen is a young woman forced into drug and alcohol rehabilitation. While in rehab, Gwen witnesses her roommate, Andrea, cutting herself. The following dialogue between Gwen and Andrea ensues:

Andrea: Just so you know, I wasn't trying to off myself or anything.
Gwen: Okay.
Andrea: It's just something I do sometimes.
Gwen: Doesn't it hurt?
Andrea: Feels better.
Gwen: Than what?
Andrea: Everything else.

This short exchange between these two characters beautifully summarizes the purpose of self-injury to its user. Self-injury acts as a means of managing pain, numbness, or any other intolerable feeling. It can snap the individual back into "reality," or it can assist in drawing energy away from the reality of the moment or situation. But where does this pain come from? Why would someone have such a strong need to "check out"? Many people experience pain but do not self-injure. Gwen, the lead character in the movie previously described, experiences pain that prompts her to abuse alcohol, but she does not cut. What is the significant difference between Gwen and her roommate, Andrea, that would lead one young woman to cut and not the other? Certainly someone does not just start cutting her skin without some sort of contributing factors. Of course there are contributing factors. Every human (self-injurious or not) possesses a concoction of variables that comprises his or her story. Certainly, there is agreement that a person does not become an engineer simply because he or she enjoyed playing with Legos as a child. Most would agree that other factors participated in this occupational choice. The self-injurer is no different. Each individual is unique. Therefore, it is at best difficult to point out simply one factor as a predictor or explanation for self-injury. The recipe for that particular person must be examined. This chapter will address those factors that may contribute to self-harming behavior.

BIOLOGICAL AND PSYCHOLOGICAL FACTORS

Biological considerations are certainly a part of the *why* equation. While one's biology serves as a significant contributor to personal destiny in life, it is again important to realize that biology alone cannot be blamed for a tendency toward self-injury. For example, John may be the progeny of alcoholic parents, and each of those parents come from alcoholic parents, and so on. Does this mean that John is destined to a lifestyle plagued with alcohol abuse or even addiction? Of course not! While a genetic predisposition may exist, this does not mean that John must abuse or develop an addiction to alcohol. John can make different choices. Perhaps John is raised in an environment in which alcohol is not displayed as a means for managing stress by his caregivers. Perhaps John finds other means of dealing with his own stress than using alcohol. Of course, it would be easy for John to travel down the path of his biological parents. No one is saying the path for John would be an easy switch from the path that has been cleared before him. The point is one's biological predisposition does not always determine one's future. Consequently, another point could be made that while biological predisposition is a powerful consideration, it often works in conjunction with environment. This is important when considering biological variables.

Neurotransmitters and Mood Stabilization

A very powerful biological consideration when understanding mood stabilization is the function of neurotransmitters like serotonin and dopamine. At least most of the literature agrees that serotonin is a neurotransmitter. Some of the literature says that serotonin "acts like" a neurotransmitter. There is some discrepancy in definition. For the purpose of this text, it will be referred to as a neurotransmitter.

Before discussing serotonin and dopamine specifically, a brief explanation of how a neurotransmitter affects the body is in order. Neurotransmitters are chemicals that send signals across a synapse from one neuron (otherwise referred to as a brain cell) to a receiving neuron. In effect, the purpose of the neuron is to deliver information from one cell to another. The purpose of the neurotransmitter being sent across a synapse is to hold onto the information it contains until it reaches its destination. This is how information vital to biological functioning is transported throughout the body regardless of the neurotransmitter. Other types of monoamine neurotransmitters include, but are not limited to, dopamine, norepinephrine, epinephrine (what we often refer to as adrenaline), and histamine. As just mentioned, these are monoamines, meaning they are a set of neurotransmitters that are composed of one amino group connected to a two-carbon chain. For the purpose of this chapter, a more functional definition is that these neurotransmitters are involved in brain function that involves emotion (or emotional regulation) and certain types of memory. If these types of neurotransmitters do not get to their postsynaptic destination, a likely result will be emotional dysregulation. Emotional dysregulation is often referred to as depression or anxiety.

The process through which any neurotransmitter completes its function is truly miraculous. Neurotransmitters are clustered in the axon terminal of the sending neuron before being delivered across a synapse to the receiving neuron. Once a neurotransmitter travels successfully across the synapse, receptor cells on the dendrite of the receiving neuron accept the neurotransmitter and, consequently, the information it has to deliver. A neurotransmitter is actually a messenger that suffers one of three fates: (1) It may be successfully delivered to the receiving neuron; (2) it may be destroyed by enzymes; or (3) it may be pulled back into the sending neuron by reuptake with the potential to be resent at a later time. Problems like emotional dysregulation occur if the neurotransmitter does not reach its destination.

The literature describes serotonin as "acting like" a neurotransmitter in the brain. With cells all over the brain that are receptive to serotonin, it is believed to be highly influential in a variety of biological functions. Interestingly enough, most of the serotonin in the body can be found in the intestines. Among other functions, it is involved in appetite and the regulation of sleep. It is also influential in memory making and learning. In fact, serotonin is (at the very least) indirectly related to almost all brain function that occurs in the human body.

Serotonin is also responsible for psychological functioning, particularly in regard to mood. If a correct balance of serotonin exists in the brain, the mood is regulated and the individual can move through daily functioning with an even mood. This does not necessarily mean that properly balanced serotonin leads to blind contentment. A person with balanced serotonin levels who experiences a car wreck will still be fearful at the point of impact and perhaps angry at the crumpled fender on her car. Certainly, happiness and contentment are emotions that are possible if the mood is even. However, many other feelings are available to the human experience, including anger, fear, loneliness, pain, shame, guilt, sadness, and confusion. This, of course, is not an exhaustive list but a general baseline of emotions. A proper balance of serotonin simply means that the person is better equipped to experience these feelings as they come along in life.

Difficulties arise when serotonin (or any neurotransmitter) does not reach its destination. This can happen in a variety of ways. Perhaps serotonin receptor sites are not open or the production level in the brain is impaired. Or, serotonin simply does not get to receptor sites. In any of these instances, it is believed that mood impairment or disorder may occur. Depression and/or anxiety are often believed to be the result of this impairment.

In many studies involving serotonin levels and their relationship with self-injurious behavior, there appears to be a correlation between low levels of serotonin and the habitual use of self-injury. At the time of this publication, there remains a great deal that is not understood about the relationship between levels of serotonin and the use of self-injury. However, the literature suggests that a clear relationship exists. If one is low in serotonin, the brain still seeks to maintain a balance in mood.

Many will manage mood with medical prescriptions such as selective serotonin reuptake inhibitors (SSRIs). These are more commonly referred to as antidepressants. Others may attempt to reach balance through other methods. These methods can range from the healthier end of the spectrum like appropriate amounts of exercise, meditative activities, and healthful nutrition to a potentially destructive set of behaviors like alcohol or drug abuse, binging and/or purging food, or, of course, self-injurious behavior.

Judging the type of behavior is not as important at this point as under-standing the purpose of the behavior. In an attempt to even one's mood, many different behaviors may be employed.

Dopamine, also a monoamine neurotransmitter, is responsible for a variety of essential bodily functions. It plays a vital role in gastrointestinal motility and insulin production and even acts as an inhibitor of norepi-nephrine (adrenaline) in the body. Destruction of dopamine in a part of the brain referred to as the substantia nigra can produce the symptomatol-ogy associated with Parkinson's disease. In brain function and particularly in relation to mood regulation, dopamine is related to reward-oriented behavior. When a reward is gained, dopamine is released. If an individual really likes chocolate cake, just the sight of the cake can raise dopamine levels. If the cake is not received, dopamine levels drop. Simply put, eat the cake and feel good (for a while anyway). With this example, one can understand the effects that dopamine can have on the process of addiction. Alcohol, gambling, sex, food, or anything that can result in a pleasurable return to the individual is related to the release of dopamine.

The effects of dopamine can even be found in the process of effective (or ineffective) parenting. If a child is frequently in healthy, interactive relationship with a parent or caregiver, this can have a substantial effect on neuronal processes that promote dopamine transportation. In other words, if the child is frequently talked with, touched, hugged, and played with, dopamine is released and the child receives the reward of safety and contentment in the relationship with the parent. This is the core of healthy attachment behavior between parent and child. On the other hand, if the child is rarely or never the recipient of nurturing behavior from the parent, neural connections in association with dopamine can be altered, resulting in heightened anxiety and impulsive behavior on the part of the child.

Many studies have found a connection between impulse control, anxi-ety, and self-injurious behavior. One definition of self-injury might include the impulse to commit harm to the body. Many self-injuring indi-viduals report an impulse to cut or mutilate the body that is relieved when the cut is made. This suggests that if the child does not learn to be soothed by a parent's touch, hugs, and other nurturing behaviors, anxiety will ensue. Imagine the body not receiving food for many days or even weeks. As a result, the body begins to shut down. This is an apt analogy for what happens to the neglected child. With no input to encourage soothing and calmness, the child is forced to seek other means of receiving this feeling. With enough experience in feeling pain and the ensuing analgesic effect of dopamine, it is difficult for the individual to simply turn away from the self-injurious behavior.

Depression and Anxiety

When discussing mood and, consequently, mood disorders, it is important to understand the actual definitions of these two mood states. To begin, one must refer to our first biological factor, the release of serotonin and/or dopamine, or the body's ability to transport these neurotransmitters throughout the body. With dysregulation, mood states like depression and anxiety can creep into one's emotional state.

Depression is an encompassing term that actually can be defined by several different diagnoses including disruptive mood dysregulation disorder, major depressive disorder, dysthymia, premenstrual dysphoric disorder, substance-/medication-induced depressive disorder, depressive disorder due to another medical condition, other specified depressive disorder, and unspecified depressive disorder. This extensive list is not intended to overwhelm the reader with in-depth phraseology but simply to briefly describe that the term "depression" possesses many different avenues for clinical exploration. "The common feature of all of these disorders is the presence of sad, empty, or irritable mood, accompanied by somatic and cognitive changes that significantly affect the individual's capacity to function" (DSM-5, 2013, p. 155).

Anxiety, like depression, is all-encompassing. In a single word, anxiety summarizes a set of psychological states (potentially influenced by biological factors) that include several diagnoses. Again, a list will be provided not with the intent to impress the reader with scientific terminology but to impress upon the reader that anxiety can be a complex state that has many different veins of inquiry. Anxiety-associated diagnoses include separation anxiety, selective mutism, phobias, social anxiety disorder, panic disorder, generalized anxiety disorder, and substance-/medication-induced anxiety disorder. An interesting note about anxiety disorders in the DSM-5 is that they are listed in order of developmental level or age. Separation and selective mutism are related to childhood anxiety, while generalized anxiety is typically identified in adults. Anxiety and its effects on behavior will be discussed in the following paragraphs.

Anxiety disorders are characterized generally as sharing features of fear and anxiety. These are different. Fear is present in the moment. One could also state that fear is tangible. Anxiety refers to anticipating a future threat, perhaps a threat that may not exist as of yet. Anxiety is less tangible. If an individual is walking through the woods and comes upon a bear, a very tangible fear is present. This fear will prompt how the individual will proceed from the point of experiencing the bear. Should the individual run, play dead, climb a tree, or stand still? Of course, education about bears and their behavior would be useful in this case, but even if it is incorrect, a direct action can occur as a result of the fear. Anxiety is anticipating that a bear will appear at some point. This anxiety may even exist in a stretch of woods where a bear would not be present. However, the anticipation exists anyway. And, due to an excess of anticipating an event that may or may not happen, the individual develops a set of thoughts that may be maladaptive or even psychologically damaging. For example, "I am haunted by bears and they intend to get me," or, "As soon as I enter this forest, I am dead."

There are times when anticipating a problem or set of circumstances is good. When one is planning a party, it is a good thing to anticipate that if a certain number of guests attend, a certain number of refreshments will be needed. It is even better to plan for more guests to arrive than initially anticipated. It was a smart decision to have extra refreshments on hand. A problem arises when one is in a perpetual state of anticipation. This creates anxiety. Anxiety often promotes lack of movement or movement that possesses no purpose. Interestingly enough, when an individual can be in the moment and aware of present state of being, anxiety can dissipate. For example, when a track athlete is waiting for her meet later in the day, she may feel anxious. Throughout the day, the athlete may imagine not running fast enough or forgetting how to get in her stance at the starting line. Right up until the actual event occurs, the athlete may have butterflies in her stomach. After the gun has sounded and she is running against her competition, she is now focused on running and, almost magically, the anxiety disappears and is replaced with immediate feelings associated with breathing rapidly, strategizing how to move around her opponent, or even the lactic acid building in her legs. All of these are feelings based in the immediate experience. These sensations are not based in anticipation but on the here and now. To follow this logic, if one is operating in the immediate moment, there is no room for anxiety and the next right course of action will be apparent. This is a fairly simple concept, but not an easy one. It is, at best, difficult to perpetually live in the moment as a human being. Some anxiety will exist for everyone. The question at hand is, "How will anxiety be handled?"

The Brain

The discussion up to this point has revolved around monoamine neurotransmitters and their respective effects on emotional regulation. Of course, these neurotransmitters are agents of brain function. The role of the brain and, even more specifically, the limbic system cannot be overstated when conceptualizing reasoning for self-injurious behavior. A brief description of some key structures in the brain will be provided before an explanation of their roles in emotional regulation. For the purposes of this chapter, the brain can be divided into three distinct sections or lobes: the cerebrum, the cerebellum, and the brain stem.

The Cerebrum

The cerebrum or cerebral cortex is the large portion of the brain located toward the top of the skull. This part of the brain is what most perceive when they hear the word *brain*. It is composed of the frontal, parietal, occipital, and temporal lobes.

The frontal lobe lies in the front of the brain. It is the largest of the cerebrum's lobes. It is primarily responsible for planning, reasoning, and some aspects of speech. The frontal lobe also houses the precentral gyrus, which contains neurons that travel all the way to the spinal cord. These neurons influence different groups of muscles. It also houses the postcentral gyrus, which receives input from the skin. The frontal lobes are the part of the brain where most purposeful behavior begins. When a person follows directions, balances a checkbook, or tells a great joke at a party, this is the part of the cerebrum that is largely responsible for these tasks being completed.

The parietal lobes of the cerebrum can be found at the top of the cerebrum. Like the postcentral gyrus found in the frontal lobes, the parietal lobes also receive data from the skin. Touch and sensation information is processed here including heat, cold, pressure, and position of the body in space. The parietal lobes communicate closely with the primary motor area, which is in charge of voluntary action.

The occipital lobes lie in the back of the cerebrum, just above the cerebellum. Here, sensory information from the eyes is processed and interpreted. The occipital lobes are also referred to as the visual cortex. Damage to this part of the brain can result in vision problems or even blindness even if the rest of the visual system is undamaged.

The temporal lobes can be found on the sides of the cerebrum just above the ears. This part of the cerebrum is responsible for hearing, speech perception, and some kinds of memory. This is where auditory impulses from the ears are processed. Steven Pliszka (2006), author of *Neuroscience for the Mental Health Clinician,* sums up the function of the cerebrum by stating, "If the frontal lobes are involved in doing, then the occipital, temporal, and parietal lobes are involved in perceiving and processing" (p. 16).

The Cerebellum

The cerebellum can be found behind and below the cerebrum. This part of the brain is responsible for posture, balance, and coordination. While the frontal lobes of the cerebrum are responsible for managing voluntary motion, these learned skills are perfected in the cerebellum. In other words, this part of the brain is not responsible for initiating movement, but its contribution through information it receives through the spinal cord is imperative in voluntary motion. Damage to this part of the brain can result in difficulty with equilibrium and balance, as well as fine motor functioning. One will not perfect riding a bicycle, driving a car, or even walking without the significant contributions of the cerebrum.

Brain Stem

The brain stem, which is found beneath the cerebrum and directly in front of the cerebellum, looks very much like a stalk. The stem is the gateway to the spinal cord. This is the oldest and most basic part of the brain, referred to as the reptilian brain. This part of the brain manages very basic functions in the body like sleeping and waking, digestion and elimination of waste, blood pressure, consciousness, heart rate, and body temperature. The brain stem is responsible for maintaining functions essential to survival. This structure cannot afford to focus on "extracurricular" activities like thinking. Imagine making out a grocery list, petting the dog, and maintaining heart rate all at the same time. Of course this would make day-to-day living laborious if not impossible. Involuntary functioning like breathing and heart rate are imperative to survival. Ultimately, the brain is concerned with survival first and foremost.

The Limbic System

At this point, the reader may be grasping to find the relationship between self-injurious behavior and some of the major structures of the brain. A description of the major structures of the brain is necessary prior to describing the next portion of the brain, the limbic system. It is important to note that the limbic system is comprised of many structures. For the purpose of this chapter, descriptions of some structures of the limbic system and their respective processes will be provided.

In a normal reaction to input or stimuli, the thalamus, the cerebral cortex, the amygdala, the hippocampus, and the brain stem all work in symbiosis. The thalamus is a symmetrical structure that can be found between the cerebrum and the brain stem. One of its main functions is to send sensory input to the cerebral cortex. The cerebral cortex is the gray matter that makes up the outer layer of the cerebrum. This portion of the brain is rich in sensory tissue that plays a key role in making memories. Once input comes through the sensory organs, the thalamus determines if any danger is present as a result of the input. Then the prefrontal cortex thinks through the input and determines the next course of action. Once the course of action is determined, the prefrontal cortex, which is part of the frontal lobe or "thinking" part of the brain, sends information to the amygdala. The amygdalae are two almond-shaped structures found in the temporal lobes. These structures are responsible for making informed decisions and forming an appropriate and proportionate emotional response. Then the hippocampus stores the input for future use. In effect, the memory of the input or experience can be put to use later if all goes well. Furthermore, the brain stem will likely not need to be engaged, saving the individual the stresses of cortisol and epinephrine release.

For example, a person is walking down a lonely street and hears the sound of footsteps behind him. Before he knows it, the individual feels the blow of a blunt instrument (the butt of a pistol) on his back. He turns around and sees that another man intends to rob him. The cerebral cortex takes in all of the tactile data. The thalamus determines that this is indeed a dangerous situation. The prefrontal cortex quickly thinks through the danger and determines that the individual should raise his hands to the air and cooperate with the robber's demands. The robber reaches around to the individual's back pocket, takes his wallet, and runs off. The hippocampus stores this information, which can be recalled at a later time if such a dangerous situation should arise.

In a traumatized brain, this process is thwarted. In this example, the individual is approached by his girlfriend from behind. In an attempt to playfully surprise him, she jumps on his back and screams as she does so. The thalamus interprets this input as a danger. The prefrontal cortex is passed up altogether, preventing a thought on how to approach the situation or rely on past experience. The amygdala releases a disproportionate amount of emotion. As a result, the young man flings his girlfriend from his back. This engages the brain stem and the sympathetic nervous system, which is responsible for the fight-or-flight response. An infusion of cortisol and epinephrine (also known as adrenaline) is released. Consequently, the heart rate and blood pressure rise and sweat begins to pour. Upon noticing this is his girlfriend, he is still agitated and yells at her for her behavior. Perhaps he even walks away from her or raises his hand in a defensive but violent gesture. This limbic response occurs in an attempt to protect the individual. The result is often shame and confusion due to behavior that the young man could not have imagined he would display.

Meanwhile, at a later, unrelated event, someone puts a hand on the young man's shoulder or someone whispers in his ear. This sets the individual into an emotional explosion. An onslaught of emotion pours out that is disproportionate to the input being received (e.g., a hand on the shoulder or a whisper to the ear). The important point is that the prefrontal cortex is left out of the process. Consequently, no thought about logical action can be employed. Furthermore, when traumatic events occur to a child whose hippocampus is still not fully developed, memory cannot be stored. Experience cannot become wisdom. The child who becomes an adolescent and later an adult does not learn that events are not necessarily dangerous. Consequently, the individual in question is more often than not operating out of a place of emotional dysregulation and perpetual stress.

In early childhood development, if the child suffers abuse or even neglect, the brain is altered in exactly the way just described. However, it is not the executive functioning of the frontal lobes that is damaged (unless of course this part of the brain suffers a physical trauma due to some kind of contact). Many question the intelligence of an individual who cannot seem to avoid inappropriate behavior in response to what would appear to be benign stimuli, nor do the parietal, temporal, or occipital lobes suffer the consequences of this trauma reaction. In fact, in a state of calm, the individual appears to be capable of logical reactions to stressful events. The individual has intact sensory organs. Furthermore, he or she can even describe the appropriate way to respond to stressful situations. However, when a stressful situation occurs, the individual is caught in a loop of disproportionate and often inappropriate reaction without the benefit of thinking through the stressful stimuli. This often appears to be stubbornness or defiant behavior when in actuality it is the result of an overtaxed limbic system. Bruce Perry et al. (1995) propose that the most important purpose of neuronal connection is the ability to change as a result of input. This constant charge for adaptation allows the body to survive. Ultimately, the brain is concerned with survival and will surpass any thought process to maintain it.

ENVIRONMENTAL FACTORS

When discussing the effects of biological factors on self-injury, it would simply be easier if people, or more specifically the brain, changed in a biological vacuum. Simply add a few drops of water and the human brain becomes healthy or unhealthy. Unfortunately, this is not the case.

The brain, while clearly possessing its mechanisms and processes, requires input from the environment in order to develop. It is an experiential organ.

As a case in point, when an 18-year-old leaves the house for the first time to attend college, the military, or his or her first job, does this individual instantly know how to pay rent, shop for groceries, or complete a job application simply because age 18 has arrived? "Poof! You are 18. Now you know how to function in the world!" This teenager hopefully has received some appropriate experience that will assist in functioning more efficiently in the world. Or, sometimes, she or he is not provided with age-appropriate challenges to prepare for the realities of independent living. A rude awakening often awaits these young people. The brain is similar in that it requires experience. It cannot be expected to instantly handle abstract concepts. It requires training. Various brain scan studies have shown that the brain does change as a result of age, experience, or even biological factors like disease and trauma. Studies have also shown that self-injury is more prevalent among those individuals who have experienced insecure attachments, forms of abuse, parent neglect, or peer victimization. In fact, biology and environment are always working in conjunction with one another. While biological factors have provided the structural bones in one's development, environmental factors provide the life blood and tissue.

Insecure Attachment

Nonsuicidal self-injury is ultimately related to emotional regulation. Put simply, feelings arise, the individual does not have a model for handling them, and something must be done to manage them. Consequently, the individual cuts him- or herself and experiences relief. As previously stated, this process has diminishing returns in that the individual never learns from experience in life. Wisdom cannot be gained. The person simply relies on the same method of affective coping that more often than not promotes an environment of shame and secrecy. Unfortunately, the concept that time heals all wounds does not apply to the self-injurer. For one to adapt to feelings like pain, loneliness, anger, and shame, the knowledge must be in place that these feelings can be experienced and, subsequently, survived. Secure attachment plays a significant role in this knowledge.

As an infant, it is imperative for a child to experience a secure environment in which to grow. This seems to go without saying. However, this need is not limited to the physical well-being of the child, but the emotional and cognitive well-being as well. Food and shelter are a start, but regular attention to the infant's emotional needs is equally vital. A secure attachment between the parent and child will promote the development of emotional regulation and the ability for the child to eventually self-soothe.

Before self-soothing can occur, children must first know comfort from an outside source (i.e., the parent) before they can be expected to comfort themselves or manage their emotions. The parent-child relationship is the first model for this important step in cognitive and emotional development alike. If the parent provides caring, which is displayed through hugs, kisses, cuddling, and talking, the child can begin to develop a sense of self-concept and self-worth.

Positive attachment behaviors precede the child developing skills necessary to emotional management. So, how is attachment attained? It is relatively simple (although not always easy, perhaps). Attachment behaviors require the parent or caregiver to engage with the child. Another way of putting it is for the parent to "be there" for the child. For most, this is as natural as rainfall. Picking up a baby, stroking her or his back, playing with her or him, or exchanging cooing and even incoherent gibberish together is the avenue toward solid attachment behavior. Stanley Greenspan (1993), author of *Playground Politics* and other seminal developmental texts, referred to the concept of "floor time" when working with parents needing guidance on raising their children. Even as the child ages, spending a certain amount of time engaged in play and following the child's lead for a designated amount of time promote a sense of emotional stability.

In effect, the child also learns how to ask for what he or she needs through the attachment relationship. Even an infant who has not yet mastered language can communicate his or her need for comfort and nurturance through laughing, cooing, and even crying. The parent will attend to these needs, teaching the child social skills that will pay dividends later in life. The ability to seek out others to process or talk through problems or feelings begins with this primary attachment relationship. If this attachment is successful, the individual can be expected to grow into a self-aware and emotionally regulated individual with a sense of self and ability to seek out healthy remedies to feelings like loneliness, sadness, and anger.

Meanwhile, if secure attachment is not achieved, the opposite can be expected in the child. The primary caregiver is responsible for providing the child with a guide, a safe place in which feelings can be tested and self-regulation can begin. If the child does not receive this opportunity, there is no barrier or range in which feelings may be placed. When an infant drops her or his bottle and begins to cry and reach for the object, it is as if she or he is saying, "Please comfort me so that I may learn what it means to feel soothed." The experience of comfort from another teaches the child how to soothe her- or himself. One day, when an exam is failed, a date is cancelled, or a game is lost, the individual will know how much and at what intensity to assign emotion to the event. Without these early attachment experiences, the child does not learn to emotionally handle these life situations. An infinite emotional investment, which feeds into a sense of self-worth, may be spent on a lost football game or an unsuccessful dance recital. As a child becomes an adolescent, it is not possible to simply learn how to regulate the feelings that accompany life events by observation of others or reading from a book. This kind of learning requires contact with a caregiver from an early age. As a teen becomes a young adult, the individual is at an extreme disadvantage. Observing peers capable of managing emotions and knowing that she is not capable of the same can promote external soothing techniques like self-injury.

If the attachment behavior is reasonably simple to understand and even pleasurable, what prevents many children from receiving it? The answer to this question is dependent to some extent on what the caregiver brings to the relationship. In some instances, perhaps the parents or caregivers have not been exposed to attachment behaviors themselves. If one does not receive the benefits of an engaged and interactive environment, it can be difficult to pass along that which has not been received. Perhaps the parent is dealing with his or her own emotional challenges. These challenges can range from grief reactions to depression or alcoholism.

Abuse and Neglect

Of course, abusive relationships also promote poor emotional coping skills. If a child is emotionally, physically, or sexually abused, that child to some extent still wants to please the abusive caregiver. This individual is all the child knows. She is totally dependent. By nature, she loves the parent or caregiver, and when pain is distributed to the child, pain is interpreted as love. The child wants to believe that the parent has her best interests at heart. Consequently, if the parent is hurting her, she believes she is doing something wrong. In the child's mind, it is not the fault of the abusive caregiver, but her own. She cannot trust the abuser with the feelings that she no doubt feels like shame, pain, fear, or anger, so she takes those feelings inward.

It would be a mistake to state that everyone who uses self-injury as a coping skill suffered abuse at the hands of a parent or caregiver. Self-injury in some way is a result of poor affective coping. Adolescence is a tumultuous time for anyone. This is a time in life when the individual is developing competence in social, academic, and extracurricular arenas simultaneously. The individual's brain is gaining experience in handling a variety of situations that involve multiple opportunities for emotional regulation. The adolescent needs to develop independence but also needs the freedom to run back to the caregiver for support and guidance. Often this guidance is not in the form of advice but presence. The adolescent needs to know that the parent can take what he or she has to dish out—in other words, that the parent can be trusted. The adolescent can have a variety of feelings and reactions knowing that the parent can be trusted to act accordingly by providing a shoulder to cry upon, appropriate limits, or a listening ear. If the parent is involved in his or her own difficulties and unable or unwilling to be invested in the child's process, from the child's perspective, this parent cannot be trusted.

This lack of trust can be in reaction to a parent who loves and is clearly invested in the child's well-being but is simply not present. Perhaps this parent works multiple jobs to bring home enough money to support the family. Or, the parent or caregiver works in a highly lucrative occupation that requires a great deal of time and effort. The parent can also be perceived as ill-equipped by the child. Depression, mental illness, alcoholism, divorce, and the death of a loved one are all situations in which the child may perceive that the parent simply has no attention to give.

And, in many instances, the child may be correct in this assumption. Research suggests that where there is self-injury, there likely exists at least some family relational difficulty. As this is such a frustrating behavior, much of the research has shown that there is often an abundance of negative affect being shown toward the self-injurer, as well as a dearth of positive affect. Self-injury occurs both in families that possess love and supportive tendencies and families that expose children to abuse and intense neglect. The common variable is the child's perception of who is capable of being trusted. If there is no one to trust, feelings must be taken inward as there is nowhere else for them to go.

WHAT DOES SELF-INJURY ACCOMPLISH?

Ultimately, nonsuicidal self-injury provides soothing to a distressed brain and limbic system, as well as control in an environment that often promotes chaos. When a situation possesses affect that is seen as intolerable, the cut is made and soothing begins. But self-injury can serve in more ways than soothing. In the case of abuse, where pain is often perceived as love, self-injury serves as a means of self-punishment. Self-injury serves as a method of dissociating from the current situation. As previously stated, this behavior can provide an escape from feelings too intense to realize. However, self-injury can also serve to bring someone back into a state of the present. Many self-injurers will report that a cut can drown out a sense of numbness. When the individual feels nothing, self-injury can provide a sense of ground-edness. The pain provides something tangible when every other source of input yields no affect.

Furthermore, self-injury can serve as a means of communication. It is important to remember that feelings are often too intense to experience. If the inexperienced individual is faced with too many feelings at one time, the most likely result will be a shutdown or dissociation. Unfortunately, when the individual is not equipped with the understanding that feelings cannot genuinely harm him or her, he or she shuts them out before they ever surface. In this instance, feelings are simply too threatening. The self-injury provides a safe haven and keeps the feelings at bay. Consequently, the self-injurer might display his or her most recent cuts when asked the question, "How are you feeling?" The depth, length, number of cuts, and the type of instrument used might provide profound insight into the intensity and status of the individual's affective world.

CONSEQUENCES OF SELF-INJURY

Some might believe the greatest consequence of self-harming is cosmetic. In one instance, a young woman shared that her mother's main concern with her daughter's self-injurious behavior was that no one would marry her due to "all of the scarring." In fact, scars and active wounds can serve as a source of shame for many who engage in self-injurious behavior. Open wounds are to be taken seriously to avoid infection.

However, the greatest consequence of self-injury may not be the cuts themselves. In reality, the cuts are but a symptom of something greater. If self-injury provides a buffer to the outside world and the potential for emotional involvement in it, then the self-injurer is missing out on a great deal of living. If depression and anxiety are states of being more than an actual affect, and affect is evidence of living, the self-injuring individual is operating from a place of loneliness and discontentment. The greatest consequence of self-injury might involve not knowing how to handle life on its terms. People must grieve, lose, win and experience anger and hurt, as well as joy, to truly say, "I have lived." The self-injurer misses out on this experience.

Those who self-injure often report a sense of feeling different than their contemporaries. While cutting provides a sense of soothing and calmness, it also can be a source of tremendous shame and guilt about the behavior. "Why can't I be like everyone else?" Self-injury is the result of being offered few, if any, healthy emotional coping skills. The self-injurer does not know a better way to manage his or her emotional life. Consequently, the behavior will not be given up without substantial resistance and for good reason. There are likely many reasons to defend this bit of respite. One will likely not give up a behavior like self-injury until a more facilitative behavior can be discovered.

CONCLUSION

This chapter has provided the reader with some contributing factors to the behavior of self-injury. In detailing some of the neurological, psychological, and environmental contributors to this behavior, the reader can better understand some of the very real factors that prevent the self-injurer from simply stopping the behavior. Through gaining some perspective on these very complex processes, perhaps the reader may also gain some hope in knowing the factors that will contribute to the process of change, as well as the process through which this behavior has manifested.

CHAPTER 3

Self-Injury and Other Conditions

Nonsuicidal self-injury (NSSI) has long been the source of misunderstanding and confusion among family, friends, and even professionals. How does NSSI manifest itself? What are the contributing factors? How does the individual manage it? These are complicated concepts. A particularly confounding variable with NSSI is its comorbidity, or coexistence, with other conditions. It can be difficult to grasp how NSSI can coexist with issues such as suicidal behavior and eating disorder and yet be a separate concern altogether. Common questions can be "Isn't self-injury just an attempt at suicide?" or "How are self-injury and eating disorder similar? They appear so different." In fact, NSSI can look much like suicidal behavior. And while NSSI and eating disorder appear so different in terms of their application, they serve very similar purposes. Interestingly enough, NSSI has numerous commonalities with suicidal behavior, eating disorder, and substance abuse.

Before examining comorbidity with these conditions, the relationship of self-injury with trauma must be examined. While the title of this book refers to cutting and self-harm, one could easily write a book on trauma symptomatology and how self-injury and all previously mentioned self-harming behaviors relate to it. As the intermingling relationships between trauma and each of these self-harming behaviors are investigated, terms like "self-regulation" and "dysregulation" will begin to surface. A definition for these terms must (and will) be provided to best understand how self-harming behaviors play such a meaningful part in the emotional life of those who employ them. Needless to say, confusion and misunderstanding can abound. The purpose of this chapter is to outline the connections between NSSI and these previously mentioned conditions.

SELF-INJURY AND TRAUMA

While self-injury has been noted, cataloged, and theorized for decades, until the late 1980s, it was considered mainly in a few domains. For one, it was (and is) recognized for its association with borderline personality disorder. The literature also has acknowledged associations between self-injury, psychosis, and organic conditions. However, in the late 1980s and into the 1990s, a new direction emerged in the focus of self-injury research; that focus was on self-injury and its relationship to childhood and adult trauma. A great deal has been revealed on the long-term effects of trauma on survivors. The function that self-injury serves in trauma survival is now viewed with more clarity. Those who study self-injury now know that it can play an integral part in managing trauma and its aftermath.

Before going too far into how self-injury and trauma are connected, a definition of trauma is in order. Interestingly enough, trauma means "wound" in the Greek translation. This certainly makes sense of the medical definition of trauma. When an individual is rushed to the emergency room with a gunshot wound, it is not difficult to imagine that this person has suffered a trauma to the body. Often, it is more difficult to understand that an individual has suffered trauma through experiences that do not necessarily leave physical evidence. For example, active duty personnel may witness the death of comrades and/or enemy forces while in combat. While no physical harm may have fallen to these individuals, a psychological and emotional trauma has occurred. In another example, an 8-year-old girl may observe her 15-year-old brother being beaten by their father on numerous occasions. While this child has not suffered a physical trauma, she experiences overwhelming psychological and emotional trauma through observation.

Trauma may be broadly defined as an emotional and psychological response to an overwhelming event like a car crash, rape, or natural disaster. One may survive a significant event like a car crash and have little, if any, psychological or emotional distress, while another individual may suffer a similar event but be significantly impacted. Difficulty arises when the emotions and thoughts associated with an event become too overwhelming to manage psychologically for the individual. When that individual becomes overwhelmed, the stress is immense and, at a point, intolerable. In this case, the individual seeks to manage this intolerable affect.

Self-injury can assist with the management of intolerable affect. Connors (1996) proposed that self-injury served two different objectives in victims of childhood trauma. The first objective is a reenactment of the trauma that was suffered. The rationale is that through unconscious reenactment, the individual can gain some perspective on the trauma and communicate it internally while attempting to sort it out. In other words, the individual is trying to make sense of the trauma. The second objective is to express the feelings associated with the trauma. Feelings such as rage, anger, shame, and pain can be expressed in the safest capacity known to the individual. In this instance, the individual likely finds external expression of these feelings to be unsafe. Self-injury provides a safe expression as it is directed inwardly. The individual need not worry about how the expression will be perceived or interpreted as she or he is the only one who experiences it.

Smith, Kouros, and Meuret (2013) have reviewed research that supports Connors's observations about the purposes of self-injury and its relationship to trauma. A link between trauma and NSSI certainly exists. In particular, there appears to be a connection between childhood traumatic experiences and NSSI. To further explain this concept, attachment between a child and caregiver must be briefly outlined. When an infant reunifies with his or her mother and has developmentally appropriate attaching behaviors like cooing, talking with the infant, making silly faces, and laughing with one another, endogenous opioids are released in the brain, and the infant feels a sense of calm and soothing. When these opioids are withdrawn from the infant as a result of feelings of abandonment or perceived withdrawal from the parent, distress sets in, inhibiting the infant's ability to learn self-regulation. When this individual experiences separation or abandonment from others, this distress reappears. Survivors of childhood abuse may have experienced this process. The individual may experience soothing and regulating sensation from the use of NSSI and other similar behaviors like disordered eating and the use of mind-altering substances.

A history of abuse, particularly sexual abuse, seems to indicate that self-injury would serve a very necessary function in human development, self-regulation, and self-soothing. However, it would be a mistake to assume that the presence of NSSI always indicates sexual or physical abuse. A parent or caregiver who simply is not present or even neglectful may hasten the use of coping skills such as NSSI. Genuine abandonment or neglect or the child's perception of abandonment or disconnection from the caregiver is a vital consideration when conceptualizing the development of these behaviors.

This brings to light another critical point that merits further research. NSSI may not always arise from childhood trauma. In previous studies, approximately 50 percent of those who used self-injury reported childhood abuse, leaving others who reported using self-injury without an account of childhood abuse (Gratz, 2003). Members of the gay, lesbian, bisexual, and transgendered communities have reported the use of NSSI as a result of managing the psychological and emotional effects of discrimination. The prevalence of NSSI among military personnel and veterans enrolled in college settings has been studied. These are just a few examples of studies that indicate the use of NSSI as a coping skill well into adult life. More research is needed to make more conclusive statements.

A discussion of self-injury in relation to trauma would not be complete without addressing the concept of dissociation. Dissociation could be considered a crucial psychological tool used to separate the individual from an overwhelming trauma. NSSI, while used for the purposes of affect or feelings management, can also be used for the purposes of combating feelings of numbness. In other words, NSSI can be used as a grounding technique. Self-injury brings the individual back into the here and now. Many individuals who report using self-injury will indicate a sense of being outside one's own body or feeling disconnected from an experience in which the individual is currently engaged. Steven Levenkron (1998) referred to this as dissociative self-injury. Some will report having a sense of amnesia after the self-injury. The individual may be surprised that there is an indication of a cut, burn, or disfigurement as he or she does not remember committing the act.

The prevalence of trauma when discussing self-harming behaviors cannot be overstated. As previously mentioned, trauma has many methods of invading the life of an individual and tampering with naturally developed means of self-soothing and self-regulation. While this chapter discusses the coexistence of self-injury with other self-harming behaviors, it is advised that the reader consider the existence of trauma in any combination of these behaviors. The research indicates that trauma must always be considered when discussing self-injury, eating disorder, or substance abuse.

SELF-INJURY AND SUICIDAL IDEATION

When discussing these two variables, NSSI and suicidal behavior, it is advisable to first remember their very different, respective definitions. Nock and Favazza (2009) define NSSI as deliberate self-harm or mutilation to a body part with the absence of suicidal intent. Meanwhile, suicidal behavior is the expressed desire and accompanying behavior of attempting to end one's life. A further distinction is in suicidal ideation in which the individual participates in the act of thinking about suicide without actually committing it. At first glimpse, these respective definitions provide a clear difference between them. One, NSSI, suggests that the individual conducts self-harming acts to the body but does not commit the act with the intent of death, while suicidal behavior means that the individual intends to end his or her life. By stating these definitions, it would appear that these behaviors are distinct and separate. However, the literature suggests that where NSSI is found, suicidal behavior is sure to be present as well.

In an exhaustive review of the literature regarding self-injury and suicidal behavior, Hamza, Stewart, and Willoughby (2012) found a consensus among researchers that a prior history of self-injury is a strong predictor of suicide attempts. Individuals who participated in inpatient treatment and who reported the use of self-injury were at a greater risk for death by suicide at the conclusion of or during treatment. In a study by Claes et al. (2010), individuals who engaged in self-injury were significantly more likely to have made a suicide attempt than those who did not participate in self-injurious behavior. In fact, NSSI was a better predictor of suicidal behavior than individual depression, hopelessness, or even surviving child abuse. This (and a plethora of other studies) suggests that NSSI not only goes hand in hand with suicidal behavior but that NSSI is the greatest predictor of it. Research makes it difficult to acknowledge the existence of one of these behaviors without considering the existence of the other.

However, while there exists a clear link between NSSI and suicidal behavior, there is research that suggests that each of these behaviors can also exist independent of one another. For example, in one study, adults who attempted suicide reported greater levels of depression, suicidal ideation, and hopelessness than those individuals who participated in NSSI alone. Furthermore, individuals who reported participating in suicidal behavior also reported greater symptomatology of psychopathology than those who reported participating in NSSI only. These two studies suggest that NSSI and suicidal behavior, while certainly linked, are also stand-alone behaviors.

With what might appear to be conflicting data, what is one to think about the relationship between NSSI and suicidal behavior? Should NSSI be seen as a clear predictor for suicidal behavior in which caregivers and/or professionals should anticipate only a matter of time before the self-injurer becomes a suicide attempter? Or, conversely, should these be seen as strictly different issues that likely exist separately from one another and only join through a series of variables that research has not yet revealed?

Again, confusion can abound. The answer is likely not found in a vacuum. Theories exist that attempt to explain answers to these questions.

One theory, referred to as the gateway theory, suggests that NSSI and completed suicide exist on a continuum of behaviors with NSSI being at one far end and completed suicide occupying the other end of the continuum. This theory also holds that NSSI would precede a completed suicide with self-injurious behaviors serving as a gateway to more severe suicidal behavior. Each possesses similar qualities in that they are each self-injurious and a conscious intent to commit either or both acts exists.

Another theory that possesses similarities to the previously mentioned gateway theory is Joiner's theory of acquired capability for suicide. In this theory, Joiner also believes that self-injurious behavior precedes suicidal behavior. In this model, the individual must first overcome the fear of committing the act of suicide. Self-injurious acts like cutting or burning can serve this purpose. However, according to Joiner, other acts can satisfy this need, including drugs and alcohol or dysfunctional eating.

There also exists a third-variable theory in which the relationship between suicidal behavior and self-injury is more tenuous than previously described. In this model, research supports that a third variable frequently comes to the forefront when suicidal behavior and self-injury coexist. The prevalence of psychiatric diagnoses or even psychological distress is often reported when both variables are present. This suggests that if an individual suffers from a psychiatric disorder (the primary variable) like borderline personality disorder or major depressive disorder, then secondary variables like suicidal behavior and self-injury possess a greater possibility of existing.

Each of these models provides compelling, new conceptualizations toward the coexistence of self-injury and suicidal behavior. However, the small amount of research to support any one of these theories suggests that conclusions cannot yet be finalized. Hamza, Stewart, and Willoughby (2012) suggest an integrated model, which takes some piece of each of these theories into account. The greatest statement is that an "indirect path" (p. 492) exists between self-injury and suicidal behavior. One conclusion that can be taken from the research discussed is that each behavior should be taken seriously. As will be discussed later in this chapter, the current literature suggests that self-injury serves as a means to soothe the individual. As garnered from the definition provided in Chapter 1, NSSI serves a purpose of medicating or soothing feelings or affect perceived as too overwhelming to experience. Clearly, if this behavior no longer provides the desired effect, the individual will likely seek other means for deadening the intolerable affect. This supports some of the previously mentioned theories. While moving down the continuum of self-harming behavior, the individual becomes desensitized to the potential pain and fear associated with suicidal behavior. This suggests that as time and habitual behavior or even addictive behavior add up, the possibility for suicide becomes more possible.

However, it is wise to consider that while the individual is self-injurious, that does not necessarily suggest that suicide is immediately eminent. An individual can participate in NSSI for years before suicidal behavior becomes a possibility. Self-injury can be seen as an acquired behavior that serves a purpose. It provides medication for what ails the individual. However, this behavior is dysfunctional. It is not a sustainable model for mental and/or psychological health (not to mention physical health). Without changing one's form of managing the intolerable affect, it is very likely that suicidal behaviors or ideation may loom on the horizon.

SELF-INJURY AND EATING DISORDERS

While the relationship between self-injury and suicidal behavior can often prove to be confusing, the relationship between self-injury and eating disorders can be less difficult to differentiate but still promotes frustration and concern. Defining eating disorders is an extensive task. To begin, eating disorders involve anorexia nervosa, bulimia nervosa, and binge eating disorder. Anorexia nervosa involves starving oneself through denial of calorie intake, which leads to excessive weight loss. According to the National Eating Disorders Association, symptoms associated with anorexia nervosa include inadequate food intake leading to exceedingly lowered body weight, an intense fear of weight gain, and self-esteem that is overly related to body image. Additionally, anorexia can be further described as binge eating/purging type, which involves binge eating and purging behaviors within the last three months. Or, the behavior can be described as restrictive type, which does not involve binging and purging but rather restricting food intake at an often alarming level, meaning that the individual can restrict calorie intake to a very low or nonexistent level.

Bulimia nervosa involves a cycle characterized by bingeing on food and then compensating for the intake of calories by purging what is consumed. This is often accomplished by vomiting or even excessive exercise to compensate for the potential effects of the binge eating. Symptoms involve episodes of bingeing followed by purging, a feeling of lacking control during periods of the binge/purge cycle, and self-esteem that is overly related to body image. Finally, binge eating disorder is a type of eating disorder that involves binge eating without the use of purging to compensate for the bingeing behavior. The primary symptom involves eating large amounts of food without accounting or compensating for the effects of weight gain. Another notable symptom is an accompanying sense of shame and lack of control when consuming large amounts of food.

While this is hardly an extensive description of eating disorders, some common themes may be identified. Perhaps most importantly, all eating disorders involve extreme emotions, attitudes, and behaviors around maintaining a certain weight and one's relationship with food. Next, and perhaps equally important, is the shame and feelings of low to nonexistent control the individual experiences in relation to his or her use of food.

The connection between self-injury and eating disorders has been well documented since the 1980s. Since that time, the literature appears to agree that both of these behaviors serve the purpose of emotional regulation and a means of communication. In this context, emotional regulation means that the individual is able to maintain or control affect or feelings through the use of one (or both) of these behaviors. The individual experiences stimuli in the environment that provides stress. Once the stress is realized, the individual may choose a behavior to manage that stress. In this case, self-injury and/or binging and purging behaviors or denying oneself food would serve as a means of controlling feelings instigated by the environmental stressor.

In terms of communication, each one of these behaviors can be used as a means of communicating one's affective regulation. In other words, the individual can use one or both of these behaviors to describe the degree of managed feelings. This is a fortuitous place to identify that internal feelings are being communicated by external means. If the individual displays a particularly fresh and deep cut on her or his forearm, one could gather that she or he is experiencing distressing affect. The same could be said if the individual began to binge on food and then purge (i.e., throw up, exercise). If this were new behavior or if episodes of the behavior began to increase and intensify, one could reach the same conclusion as described with the incident of self-injury. In these examples, both of these behaviors are clearly used for communication and clearly both are self-harming. In fact, these behaviors may very well fulfill their purpose, emotional regulation and communication. These are worthy goals. Everyone needs a vehicle to express and feel connected. However, in the case of NSSI and eating disorders, self-harm must first be done before either of these goals may be accomplished.

The physical harm that may occur by habitual disordered eating is a topic that deserves much discussion. A variety of unfavorable consequences can result from disordered eating, ranging from tooth decay to gastric rupture while bingeing. However, this topic is beyond the scope of the chapter. Certainly, physical difficulties are worth mentioning when breaching the subject of eating disorder. But it is the emotional toll on the individual that must come first if dysfunctional eating and, consequently, unhealthy affective regulation are to change. For the purposes of this writing, the emotional well-being of the individual is the centerpiece.

SELF-INJURY AND SUBSTANCE ABUSE/MISUSE

Self-injury and illicit drug use have maintained a distinct, but elusive, relationship in terms of research since the 1980s. There appears to be a dearth of research findings connecting these two self-harming behaviors. However, the literature suggests that a connection between the two does exist. Matsumoto and Imamura (2008) suggest that self-injury may serve as a predictor of future illicit drug use. Also, the authors suggest that a commonality between self-injury and substance abuse may be deliberate self-destruction.

A general theme in the trauma literature suggests that negative effects of early experiences would indicate a greater likelihood of disruption in the capacity to develop adaptive self-regulatory activities. In other words, the individual who experiences poor attachment or perceived (or real) abandonment is at a disadvantage when learning how to manage one's emotions. The individual seeks an external form of self-regulation. This can be in the form of mind-altering substances or other self-harming activities. There is a growing body of research concerning the existence of traumatic experiences and posttraumatic stress disorder among those suffering from a diagnosable substance abuse disorder. There also exists a connection between suicidal behavior and substance abuse. In one study, 50 percent of participants recovering from substance addiction reported past traumatic events (Ouimette, Brown, & Najavits, 1998). While more research is necessary to discover the connection between self-injury and substance abuse, connections between the use of mind-altering substances and trauma clearly exist.

As previously mentioned, if self-injury and suicidal behavior can be considered as existing on a continuum with self-injury preceding suicidal behavior, then where does substance abuse and dependence fall? Substance abuse, like self-injury, can serve as a means of soothing or, literally, medicating the traumatized individual. It is important to remember that as maladaptive as self-injury may be, it serves a purpose. Perhaps mind-altering substances can serve a similar purpose, and, furthermore, maybe these behaviors can work in conjunction with one another. In any case, this further solidifies the difficulty in simply stopping these behaviors without a measurable amount of experience with more adaptive self-regulating activities. To provide some insight into how these self-harming behaviors can work in symphony with one another, consider the following case of Erica.

A Case Example

Erica is a 25-year-old female living in a sober living house. Since Erica was 19 years old, she has been to inpatient treatment for chemical dependency on four separate occasions. She has appeared to "blow off" treatment on her previous treatment stops. Prior to achieving her current sobriety, Erica's mother, father, and two sisters frequently spoke about her apparent disregard for anything other than drinking and smoking marijuana. Furthermore, the family has communicated to Erica the amount of shame she has caused the family since leaving high school. The youngest of three daughters, Erica was 6 years younger than her closest sister and 10 years younger than her oldest. In her early years, Erica remembered her mother often being sick. Her mother would often spend days in her bedroom without seeing the rest of the family. If she were to be disturbed at the wrong time, Erica's mother might lash out at her with threats of spanking her until "her legs bled" if she did not quit disturbing her mother. After some time, her mother sought psychiatric help for what appeared to be clinical depression medicated with alcohol. Her mother began taking a psychotropic medication that appeared to assist with the depression. She also stopped drinking on her own, and the family simply did not talk any further about her bouts of depression or violent outbursts.

Throughout childhood and adolescence, Erica was an excellent student and model child. She earned excellent grades and was active in sports and other extracurricular activities. Shortly after she turned 12 years old and her next oldest sister was out of the house and off to college, Erica's uncle, Jerry (her mother's brother), moved into the house, reportedly due to financial difficulties. It was explained to Erica that they needed to help her uncle until he could get back on his feet. Erica had never known her Uncle Jerry except seeing him approximately every couple of years at her grandparents' house for the holidays. He had lived in Maine with his wife and children prior to living with Erica and her parents.

One late night, while Erica was asleep in her bed, she was horrified to awaken and discover her uncle lying next to her. He proceeded to undress and rape her. In shock, Erica could only respond with her mouth agape trying to scream; however, no sound would come out. Once her uncle realized she was trying to scream, he covered her mouth. Jerry told her he did not want to hurt her and would not as long as she did not scream. As he removed his hand from her mouth, Jerry warned Erica not to share this with her parents. "They would not do anything about it and telling them would only make things worse for you," he told her. Jerry then left the bedroom and told her he would see her again at breakfast. Erica laid there all night in the fetal position fearing to move. In the morning, Erica went to her father. She fearfully shared the events of the previous night. Her father looked remorsefully at her and hugged his daughter, telling her that he loved her. She was then encouraged to get ready for school as her father "considered" how the family would handle the situation.

That night, Erica's parents asked Jerry to go out to dinner so they could sit down with their daughter. Erica's mother expressed remorse at her brother's actions and apologized for them. Then Erica's mother told her, "You have to learn to forgive your uncle. He has a terrible problem with this. That is why he lost his job and his family. We will have Uncle Jerry move into an apartment, but you have to promise that you will not tell anyone about this. If anyone found out, including your sisters, Jerry could go to jail and we can't have that happen. You have to help us with this, Erica. You just don't have any choice."

Unable to grasp what she was being told and feeling betrayed, Erica agreed to keep the secret. Weeks after that event, Erica's parents noticed small cuts on her inner thighs near her knees. Erica began cutting herself with a paring knife that she found in the back of a kitchen drawer. In the past, anytime she would reach for another utensil from that drawer, she would see the paring knife in the same position for years. No one would miss it. So she took the knife from the drawer and hid it in her bathroom cabinet. To this day, she does not know why she chose that instrument to cut herself. She later reported in treatment, while finally describing the event, that from the night her uncle raped her, she felt a scream erupt from as deep in her body as her stomach. When she would cut herself, the scream would be muffled and Erica could continue with daily life.

Erica continued to be a model student and citizen into high school. She was equally beneficent at home except that every once in a while, she would break into a fit of rage about otherwise normal situations. If she was denied going out with friends or was told to change her clothes if they were "too provocative," Erica might lash out with violent yelling and even threats of running away or hitting one of her parents. Upon witnessing this behavior, Erica's sisters chalked up her behavior to being the baby in the family and that their parents had spoiled her.

Once Erica left for college, she soon expanded an already robust habit of using marijuana. Now away from home, Erica could drink with friends without fear of being discovered by her parents. She had difficulty with nightmares and would often refuse to turn off the light in her dorm room. This promoted difficulty with roommates, and Erica soon moved from the residence hall to an apartment off campus. She did not finish her freshman year and did not return to college but elected to work for one of the local bars near campus. Here she continued drinking and employing self-injury daily.

She often called home asking for money from her parents. Setting faint boundaries of not loaning her more money until she went back to school, Erica's parents gave her the requested sum of money while sharing with Erica's sisters that they just did not know what to do with her. Her parents, particularly her mother, were obsessed with the idea of keeping track of Erica. Erica's family was aware that she had habitually used marijuana since high school and alcohol since college. Due to this, her parents have always seen her as fragile and unable to take care of herself. Her older sisters have shared in that sentiment except they were each unwilling to go on what they referred to as "Erica watch." This contributed to distance in their relationships.

Today, Erica has graduated from an inpatient chemical dependency treatment facility. With three months of sobriety, Erica has been able to confront her parents in treatment about the secret she was implored to keep nearly 13 years prior. Erica and her sisters now have a more understanding but still distant relationship. Her sisters maintain a strong bond with their parents even after knowing the truth about their uncle's sexual abuse of their sister.

This is the longest sobriety Erica has experienced. She reports that while physically she feels better than she has since she was a child, she also feels a sense of uneasiness or constant anxiety. This makes remaining sober very difficult even though she attends daily 12-step meetings, has acquired a sponsor, and is attempting to find a job. Erica also reports that she likes the idea of sober living. In most ways, her life is more consistent and predictable than it has been in years. She likes this feeling, but she also openly admits that she truly misses how marijuana and alcohol dampened her feelings of pain, guilt, anger, and shame. She does not want to drink again, but she does not trust herself to remain sober without almost constant supervision. She requests friends and family check on her frequently. This contributed to her parents' image of her as a fragile person.

Wanting to remain substance free, Erica admits that it is hard to do even though this is what she wants. Erica still uses self-injury on an almost daily basis. "I can't quite give this one up. It helps me sleep better. I also still want to scream, but nothing will come out."

Hopefully, in reading Erica's story, it is understood that she is not a youth who foolishly fell prey to the pitfalls of using drugs and alcohol. Furthermore, Erica was not cutting herself with an instrument that originally belonged to her abuser simply to gain attention from her family. It is important to see that Erica was a member of a dysfunctional family who absorbed tremendous shame about her mother's depression and alcohol abuse. The story does not provide this information, but it is possible that Erica also suffered a difficult attachment to her mother. If Erica's mother was depressed through Erica's infancy and incapable of interacting with or even seeing her for extended periods of time, Erica may not have gained the ability to self-soothe.

Then, of course, Erica suffered an overwhelming traumatic event in being raped by her uncle. To add to the pain and betrayal of the abuse, her uncle was correct when he told Erica that her parents would not do anything about it (the rape). With feelings that were too overwhelming to comprehend, Erica found means to manage her feelings through smoking marijuana, drinking alcohol, and self-injuring. Notice that even after 90 days of sobriety, new coping skills learned in treatment settings and 12-step meetings, and a genuine desire to manage her life in a more functional way, Erica still cannot stop cutting. This is not a failure on her part to finally remove all maladaptive habits. This is holding on to what she still needs to manage life's daily challenges. She is still making sense of the confusion, anger, and pain that accompanied much of her life. She has come by her coping skills honestly. They do not simply disappear like rain clouds on a sunny day but peel away like layers of an onion.

CONCLUSION

This chapter has covered the coexistence of self-harming behaviors. These behaviors often work in concert with one another. There remains a paucity of research to explain exactly how this occurs. However, it is now understood that these behaviors serve a purpose for the self-harming individual. Research has shown that self-harm, in its many forms, can look very different but actually serve a very similar purpose. The purpose is almost always self-soothing or feelings management. But also these behaviors act as a means of internally making sense of overwhelming experiences and even providing a means of communicating the affect associated with these experiences that cannot be put into words.

CHAPTER 4

Responding to Self-Injury

How can someone respond to self-injury? This is a complicated question. So much of how to respond is related to the individual's level and the quality (quality meaning assets or characteristics) of the relationship. Particularly in adolescent and teen environments, it may be particularly hard to describe one's concerns. This is a difficult time of life where expressing one's concerns and beliefs is a challenge and developmentally awkward. If a friend is committing self-injury and it appears to work for her or him, who can say the behavior should stop? If it does not genuinely harm, meaning that life is not threatened or functioning is not impaired, what leg does one have to stand on in confronting the self-injuring individual?

For parents and other authority figures, it is often hard not to see self-injury as a form of defiance. Consequently, the quality of this kind of relationship might look like a lecture or authoritative guidance that the self-injuring individual might resist altogether. In other cases, fear and confusion about the behavior can shut down communication leaving all involved hoping the behavior will simply go away. Due to several variables, responding to self-injury as a family member has its own unique concerns. Consequently, an entire section of this chapter is dedicated to the familial response to self-injury.

The reality is that a response is imperative for those concerned. Even if an individual can live a lengthy life while self-injuring, it is not as much about the cuts or scars as it is about the internal experience of this person. If self-injury is about managing feelings—a better description would be feeling avoidance—what caring individual would want that for a loved one? The compelling question is how to form an appropriate response.

Those concerned must first know how to identify self-harming behavior, particularly self-injury. The first indications of self-injury may very well be actual cuts or abrasions that are not accompanied by a viable explanation. Many who practice self-injury will have unexplained cuts on the forearms, legs, feet, or hands. Self-injurers may use a variety of places on the body depending upon their respective rituals around the behavior. For example, self-injury may be as obvious as a long, deep cut on the forearm in full view of anyone who may observe the injury. Or, some reports exist of injuries being less conspicuous like a small incision between the toes or an abrasion to the upper arm. These, of course, are examples. An individual is limited only by his or her imagination in where to commit injury to the body.

Self-injury can occur around places on the body that are more sexualized like the breasts, genitals, or buttocks. Injuries inflicted to these areas on the body may suggest abuse and/or trauma, which was discussed in Chapter 3. Likely, concerned individuals will not observe these injuries unless a common area, like a locker room, is shared or, of course, if one were in an intimate sexual relationship with the individual in question.

If an injury is observable, it is certainly appropriate to address it as a concerned individual. However, sometimes, injury is not observable as it is covered by clothing. Long sleeves in warm environments can be cause for concern. Bandages on parts of the body also may be cause for questions. Of course, some simply like wearing long sleeves, and others may simply have had a legitimate accident with a sharp object. Everyone who wears long sleeves or has a bandage is not necessarily self-injuring. However, combining these variables with an altered mood or detached involvement in a significant relationship may be indicators for concern. Perhaps visible cuts, scars, or abrasions are not visible or readily apparent, but the individual may seem less involved in relationships. An increased propensity for rageful behavior in disagreements or during other emotionally distressing events, difficulty handling anger, and genuine difficulty dealing with rejection can all be behaviors to monitor.

As discussed in Chapter 3, self-injury often accompanies other self-harming behaviors like alcohol or substance abuse. Also discussed was the all too present relationship between self-injury and eating disorders. These variables must be considered when making a determination about confronting concerns about self-injury. Another consideration is the presence of odd utensils or devices. Misshapen paper clips, exacto knives, and razor blades openly displayed can be cause for concern. Objects that simply do not appear to fit in their present environment are notable. For example, Steven Levenkron (1998), in his book *Cutting: Understanding and*

Overcoming Self-Mutilation, described a girl using the hooked portion of a belt buckle to commit self-injury. Knowing what to look for is critical. Once the concern and conviction are present, the next step is how to actually confront the behavior. That will be the focus of the rest of this chapter.

How to Respond as a Concerned Individual

As a Friend

Holly, a high school junior, has always admired her friend Karen. Karen is not only very popular at their high school, but she is an excellent student, an accomplished volleyball player, and the friend whom everyone seems to lean on. Karen is perfect from Holly's viewpoint. However, lately Karen has not been herself. Her grades have remained consistent. In fact, she appears almost panicked at the concept of dipping below a 90 percent passing rate. But she has been absent from volleyball practice on numerous occasions. Her coach, knowing that Holly and Karen are close, asks Holly if she has seen Karen.

Additionally, Karen seems to visit the girl's restroom with a concerning frequency, and she refuses to eat lunch, citing a "nervous stomach" almost every day. And, most recently, Holly has noticed uniform cuts on the side of Karen's shin. Holly has considered saying something to Karen, but she is frightened. She knows that other kids at school cut themselves. While cutting does not appeal to her, Holly is sympathetic when other kids share that their parents tried to tell them to stop it. "If parents cannot stop their own child from cutting, how am I supposed to make a difference?" Holly believes that in order to make an impact, she must have an answer for Karen about her behavior.

This story is not unusual. While it has occurred in a high school setting (where much concern around self-injury looms), Holly's fear and trepidation about confronting the behavior may just as easily be found in offices and other adult environments as it is in schools. A commonality among those concerned is a belief that they must have some kind of answer to the behavior. While answers, at times, can be helpful, they are not necessary. Having an answer is truly too much of a burden for concerned friends. In fact, a self-injuring individual may have received a great deal of advice or guidance about her or his behavior. Often, what is most impactful or appreciated is a show of care and concern. It would be completely appropriate for Holly to make the following statement:

"Karen, I am really worried about you. I notice cuts on your legs. You skip volleyball practice a lot. You are worried about grades to the point you seem to get sick over them. I think you may be cutting yourself. That really scares me and I just want you to know that if you want someone to talk with, I am willing to listen." A response similar to this one by Holly contains no advice or even a hint of an answer to the problem. Holly has simply communicated her concern and provided examples of what concerns her. She has not advised or, worse yet, chastised Karen with her confrontation. It is important to remember that someone suspected of self-injury likely knows that the behavior is concerning to others and that a common response will be, "Stop doing that." One might imagine the shame of being told to stop a certain behavior and not having an idea of how to do it. The self-injurer faces this perhaps on a daily basis. Sometimes the most helpful response is empathy and a willingness to listen without judgment.

As a Teacher or School Professional

School professionals are faced with many challenges in the course of a school day. Federal and state requirements place enormous responsibility on teachers (and other school professionals like principals and school counselors) to deliver lesson plans that measure students' understanding and implementation of a variety of concepts. Clearly, this is a teacher's primary responsibility.

Challenging student behavior is a reality of the classroom. Sometimes punitive measures like detention or doing extra work can serve as a means to deter student behavioral problems. However, in the case of a self-injuring student, punishment simply does not work. School professionals must remember that self-harming behaviors like cutting are a coping skill that this particular student has learned. In most cases, the self-injuring student is ill-equipped with other means of managing daily challenges. Frustration with a grade, another student, or the teacher's delivery of a concept that the student doesn't understand are all fertile grounds for anxiety, and that anxiety can lead to challenging behavior. While other behaviors this student displays may be difficult to manage (e.g., talking back, challenging the teacher in front of other students), it is still important to see what is happening behind the behavior.

Often with teachers, challenging behavior in the classroom is not an issue with the self-injuring student. Like many students, often (not always) the self-injurer wants to please and have a positive relationship with authority figures. The teacher may be one of the safest persons in this student's world. If this teacher is able to get in with this student and has a genuine concern, his or her response may not be terribly different than the example of the friend response previously provided. An example of an appropriate response might be, "I am worried about you. I notice that you have some cuts on your arms. It seems like you might be feeling overwhelmed and frustrated. I want you to know that while I may not understand exactly what is happening with you, I would like to. If you are willing to share what is happening with you, I would truly appreciate hearing you." Much like the previous example, teachers can share what they observe and how they feel about what they see. Another addition to this is the vulnerability of the word *appreciate*. Many times authority figures like teachers are genuinely looked up to but can be seen as unapproachable due to their position of authority. This approach can go a long way to leveling off the power differential that often exists between a teacher and student.

Sometimes, a self-injuring student presents in a challenging manner. Due to difficulty in appropriately expressing emotions and a low threshold for anxiety and frustration, self-injuring students may present as oppositional or defiant. Of course, empathy for the student's perspective must be maintained. However, this does not mean that a teacher cannot set limits in the classroom. In fact, clearly defined limits are a part of a healthy lifestyle. However, the delivery of those limits can be difficult. A stressed teacher, like anyone challenged by inappropriate behavior, may be tempted to draw a line in the sand. A common refrain might be, "If you continue to talk that way in this classroom, you are going to the principal." This is, undoubtedly, an example of a clearly set limit. However, with this particular student who is often confused by limits and does not have a solid grasp on how to handle them, this firm example may lead to further challenges.

Garry Landreth (2012), author of the book *Play Therapy: The Art of the Relationship,* developed what he refers to as the ACT model. It is described in Table 4.1.

This model has been effectively used in school environments with children across the developmental spectrum. It can be used with a variety of problem behaviors that children exhibit. This can be especially useful

Table 4.1. The ACT Model

A: Acknowledge the feeling.	*Example (Adolescent):* "I know you are frustrated with the homework assignment."
C: Communicate the limit.	"But I am not okay with being yelled at."
T: Target alternatives.	"You can choose to tell me what confuses you about the assignment."

when working with the self-injuring student. Arguably, the most important component in regard to this population is empathy or acknowledging the feeling. Often, the self-injurer does not receive empathy, but advice or correction. Second, setting a clear limit that is not charged with the teacher or school professional's own frustration can appropriately inform the student of the boundary, and lastly, the student is given choices of how to proceed. This is particularly helpful for a child or adolescent who has perhaps not received guidance in this way. Children and adolescents are frequently provided limits but may not be provided direction on what to do once a limit has been set. This section of the chapter has approached a few of the challenges that self-injuring students might present for teachers. A more comprehensive discussion about self-injury will be presented in Chapter 6 entitled "Self-Injury in School Settings."

As a Spiritual or Religious Leader

Most of the research concerning religion and self-injury focuses on delusions associated with religious overtones. This research is most frequently concerned with those participating in major self-injury or mutilation and psychosis. To date, virtually no research has been conducted on the relationship between nonsuicidal self-injury or moderate self-injury and the potential therapeutic power of religion or spirituality. What research has revealed is that many who practice moderate self-injury have experienced broken or flawed relationships from early childhood through adulthood. Many of those individuals have experienced problems with the concept of a God, a deity, or a higher power. Research also has found that those who practice self-injury are frequently challenged with perfectionism, low levels of self-forgiveness, and lofty expectations of self. These expectations often contribute to a skewed belief system of God's expectations. When perfection cannot be achieved, a greater level of self-loathing may be indicated. This is important for religious and spiritual leaders to grasp when interacting with any self-harming individual.

Conversely, self-injurers may practice a vigorous religious and spiritual life. Characteristically, these individuals may still have difficulty embracing concepts like grace or forgiveness. Furthermore, judgment from God may be an intimidating prospect. Regardless of the stance of the self-injurer about religion and spiritual values, religious and spiritual leaders have an opportunity to challenge preconceived notions about God's judgment.

Spiritual leaders like priests, ministers, imams, and rabbis can create sermons and lessons that emphasize God's care, love, and forgiveness, as opposed to God's wrath or judgment. Verses from the Bible, the Qur'an, the Torah, or other religious doctrine can be discussed from a variety of perspectives. Spiritual leaders can be available to provide guidance through abstract, religious concepts. However, these leaders should be careful when discussing the concept of sin or identifying the self-injury as sinful and being against God's will. The self-injuring individual is often already heavy with conceptions of God's opinion about her or him. Providing chastisement or judgment in an effort to convince the individual to cease the self-injury will often result in making the condition worse.

Instead, if religious leaders have concerns about someone's self-harming behavior (whether that be self-injury, an eating disorder, or addiction issues), they would be well-advised to be open to questions with answers that lack judgment about the individual's religious conviction or willingness to submit to God's will. Facilitating dialogue that promotes thoughtfulness and prayer about relationship to one's God and consideration of God's caring nature are indicated. Additionally, if possible, personal humility and vulnerability on the part of the religious leader can be helpful. For example, "I know you have been struggling lately. I have been really worried about cuts that I see on your arm. I also know you have been questioning God's purpose for you. I just want you to know that, in my past, I have had my own challenges with God's purpose for me. I am available to talk if you need me." Frequently, people in faith communities will make the response, "You are in my prayers." Instead of automatically making the statement (which is intended to be supportive), permission might be sought. For example, "Would it be alright if I included you in my prayers?" By asking permission, power is assigned to an individual who often experiences little power over any of her or his affairs. This example confronts the behavior but also allows the individual to know that struggles with God, God's will, and personal judgment are common to many people, including spiritual and religious leaders. Additionally, no judgment about the individual and his or her use of the behavior is communicated. This can make a powerful statement to the self-injuring individual that someone in her or his faith community is trustworthy.

As a Therapist

For the purpose of this section, the term *therapist* may include a variety of mental health professionals such as psychiatrists (medical doctors or MDs), licensed professional counselors (LPCs), licensed clinical social workers (LCSWs), licensed psychologists, or licensed chemical dependency counselors (LCDCs). In the therapeutic community, self-injury can be as frightening and overwhelming for the therapist as the lay person.

Until it was identified as its own distinct behavior (now described as non-suicidal self-injury or NSSI), many of those in the mental health community have confused self-injury with suicidal ideation. There is possibly no more exhausting and anxiety-provoking prospect for a therapist than a client or patient who is suicidal. Consequently, many therapists have resisted working with this population. Additionally, so much of the therapeutic community still strictly identifies self-injury with personality disorder, particularly borderline personality disorder. Borderline personality disorder is characterized by unstable mood and relationship difficulty. These qualities often emerge in therapy. Arguably, this can also be one of the more difficult client populations with which to work. The reputation of these conditions precedes them. Upon learning of either of these diagnoses, many therapists simply resist working with the challenges they represent.

Truthfully, many self-injuring clients are capable of self-maintenance through self-injury or after attempting new (and hopefully healthy) means of coping. However, therapists should plan for a certain amount of crisis intervention when working with this population. Ethical implications abound for the therapist working with a client who commits self-injury. Concerns about suicidal behavior and the potential for checking a client into a psychiatric inpatient facility or the emergency room at the local hospital are very real possibilities.

Conterio and Lader (1998) warn that working with a self-injuring client takes a certain level of tolerance and "technical finesse." Many counselors are not trained in working with this population and are not always prepared for the unique set of qualities a self-injuring client can present. Often, respect for boundaries, poor communication of emotion, and volatile shifts in mood serve to erode empathy for this particular client. Conterio and Lader (1998) also warn that self-injurious behavior can present as too gruesome for some therapists. The depth of cuts, the sight of blood, or just the concept that someone would wound her- or himself can be difficult to grasp for even the most seasoned therapist.

The therapist must have a level of self-introspection to work with this population. Short-term interventions and quick techniques such as snapping one's wrist with a rubber band or drawing a red marker line on the skin as opposed to an actual cut yield few results. The process of understanding emotions and, consequently, how to regulate them can take years of therapy. This requires an intense commitment on the part of the therapist in which regular reestablishment of relationship, confrontation, boundary setting, and emotional support are given variables in a relationship with this client.

Therapists must also be prepared to employ outside resources like support groups, group therapy, and medication management. This sort of client needs frequent support, especially in the beginning of therapy, due to an often overwhelming desire to cut. Internal resources for the client are often not yet present, and outside help is needed. Family work may also play a part in therapy depending on the client's familial situation (e.g., family estrangement, abuse situations, willingness of the family to participate, willingness for the family to participate on this part of the client, or presence of family).

Discussing the number of variables that go into working with the self-injuring client is a process that goes beyond the scope of this section of the text. However, it should go without saying that it is imperative that therapists have a solid understanding of the reasons behind the behavior. If the therapist's sole purpose is to get the client to stop self-injuring, then he or she has not encountered enough training. Furthermore, counselors must be aware of their own prejudices when encountering the self-injuring client. A therapist who thinks the client is simply using self-injury as a means of gaining attention and manipulating others while possessing no empathy for the underlining motivation may very well do more harm than good.

While it is accompanied by its own set of confounding circumstances, self-injury is but a symptom of a broader internal issue. Since the early 1990s, a variety of texts and trainings have emerged that shed a brighter light on this challenging behavior. Members of the therapeutic community are encouraged to take advantage of these resources and complete a thorough self-assessment of one's willingness to provide the required commitment to client care for this unique population.

HOW TO RESPOND AS A FAMILY MEMBER
Managing One's Own Feelings

Upon realizing that one's child, sibling, parent, or significant other is self-injuring, a variety of feelings are apparent. Disbelief and shock are quite common. It is difficult enough for most people to imagine a loved one being harmed; adding that the individual is harming him- or herself only adds to the pain and confusion. Many family members also report feelings of anger and frustration while watching the individual go from happy and vivacious to reclusive and distant. Furthermore, especially when family communication is strained and family members begin assessing their role in the situation, feelings of guilt and shame can be experienced.

At times, family members may deny the severity of the behavior. A parent may remark, "She is just doing this to get attention." In fact, there may be need for attention, and self-injury may feel like the only way to get it. Regardless, choosing to ignore the behavior will only result in further decline of the relationship and the health (both mental and physical) of the individual. The self-injury must be addressed if healthy functioning is to be restored.

Unfortunately, all too often, an adolescent will entrust a teacher, counselor, or friend with her self-harming behavior. When the suggestion is made to tell her parents, she insists that this would be a mistake and pleads for her parents not to be informed. This suggests that the adolescent fears her parents knowing about the behavior or perhaps believes they are incapable of managing the information. A troubling reality is that, many times, the family of the self-injurer is concerned with how the behavior will reflect on them. In this case, the fear that the family will not know how to handle the self-injury is fully realized. This serves to exacerbate the problem in that those who self-injure desperately need safe people to lean on. Sometimes, with assistance and guidance, the family can become a trustworthy resource. Other times, if the family is unwilling or unable to engage in new behaviors and new ways of thinking, the individual will have to seek resources elsewhere.

If family members are willing to address the reality of the self-injurious behavior, their respective roles in it, and how to make changes, there is hope that relationships can be restored and that the self-injurer will have a caring and supportive environment to thrive. However, prior to be a help to their loved one, those individuals will first have to acknowledge their own feelings about the behavior. And, once this realization is made, those individuals will have to learn how to regulate those feelings. Emotional regulation refers to being aware of one's emotional experience and then understanding how to manage those emotions. Emotional dysregulation is discussed in the self-injury literature and has been brought to the forefront due in large part to the work of Marsha Linehan (1993). Emotional dysregulation refers to the lack of emotional management. It is important to note that *management* does not mean denying feelings. It simply means having a functional or appropriate response to those feelings. While some facets of emotional regulation include neurological and genetic influences, environment must also be considered. For the self-injurer, the way to regulate emotions is to cut and the emotions are dampened leaving the individual feeling calm and that the emotional event has passed. This is not the case. Emotional residue is present until feelings are experienced and worked through. For the self-injurer, this process appears to work until another feeling arises and the process begins again creating a never-ending cycle. Family members must first understand how they regulate emotions before they can expect their loved ones to regulate theirs.

For example, beginning in the seventh grade, Sarah was painfully afraid of receiving what she considered poor grades at school. She rarely did. However, from time to time, she would receive a C in a course. When Sarah's parents received her report card, Sarah's mother would respond with a lecture about how Cs are unacceptable followed by immediately going to her bedroom to sleep in frustration. When Sarah's father would come home, he would deliver another lecture to her about her inadequate grades. He would then be unapproachable for the rest of the evening, citing his own disappointment. Sarah perceived that her parents could not handle her apparent imperfections. Consequently, she studied incessantly, receiving only As from the eighth grade on through her high school graduation and into college. While her grades became almost flawless, she also began cutting herself. From a very young age, Sarah learned that feelings were something to be avoided. Her parents communicated to her that if she did not perform exceptionally, they would first be enraged and then would detach from her. To Sarah, that was not acceptable. So, she molded herself into the image of perfection. To manage the feelings associated with maintaining that level of perfection, Sarah learned how to cut herself.

Later, when Sarah was a junior in college, she went to the campus counseling center in a state of what she referred to as an emotional breakdown. Reluctantly, after a few sessions with a counselor, Sarah agreed it would be best to contact her family and tell them what was happening with her. Her parents were in shock to learn that she was cutting herself. Both parents responded initially with what appeared to be disgust. "Why would you do that to yourself?" her mother responded, while in a family meeting at the counseling center. Both parents were clearly worried about Sarah but appeared almost afraid to hug her as if she might break under the strain of their embrace. What was particularly confusing to each of them was that their respective means of managing emotions contributed to this behavior. "I would never tell her to handle things this way! Neither of us have done anything like that before! Where did she get this!?!" exclaimed Sarah's dad. Neither parent participated in cutting, but they each possessed dysfunctional ways of communicating their feelings to their child and each other. Sarah's mother would rage and then sleep. Her father would rage and then disconnect from the family. In counseling, Sarah was learning new ways to deal with her feelings besides cutting.

Who Needs to Change?

For Sarah to trust her parents with her feelings, they would first have to learn new ways to regulate their own feelings. Sarah and her parents developed a communication cycle that promoted expression inwardly. This is particularly difficult for a child in formative developmental years. For Sarah, she learned to turn inward with her feelings at a time in life when children are learning how to appropriately express outwardly. She did not learn that lesson and had to learn it at a later time in life. The good news is she learned it, but not without costs.

Without question, those who practice nonsuicidal self-injury must learn new ways to express emotions, new coping skills, and healthy behaviors in self-maintenance. They do need to make changes. However, it is an all too common misconception that the individual is the only one in the system who must change. In reality, all who are involved must learn to change many of these same qualities.

Sarah's mother realized that she possessed a low threshold for frustration and fear. If she became overwhelmed, she slept. This was exacerbated by an addiction to painkillers for which she sought her own treatment. She realized the effect this had on Sarah. She was now aware that Sarah could not count on her to handle the turmoil that 12- and 13-year-olds experience in the process of learning how to develop coping skills for the world around them. She was now alert to the fact that Sarah could not turn to her to learn how to handle the vast array of emotions that went on internally. So, Sarah learned to handle them herself. After receiving her own help and learning how to be aware of and tolerate her own experience, Sarah's mother now was capable of being someone Sarah could rely upon emotionally. They now had a dialogue with one another. As opposed to providing a lecture followed by an exit to her bedroom and checking out with medication, Sarah's mother was now a healthy resource for her daughter.

Sarah's father was initially very slow to acknowledge his part in this elaborate drama. Like many loved ones and friends, he believed this was Sarah's problem that she must manage on her own. Consequently, when her father would say, "You can talk to me. I am here for you," she didn't believe him. This was a source of frustration for all involved. With encouragement from the family and Sarah's counselor in family meetings, her father reluctantly began seeing a therapist and acknowledging his own intolerance to emotional regulation. After several months of work, he and his daughter were beginning to have more open interactions. He began to communicate when he was frustrated, and, consequently, Sarah now believed he was an emotional support for her.

Being Genuine and Supportive

The previous vignette briefly illustrated the layers of change that often must ensue for the self-injurer to improve. Part of what changed with this family was the quality of contact made between each of them. Each family member, Sarah and her parents alike, learned to recognize their genuine experience and how to communicate to one another. This requires achieving a level of genuineness that is not always experienced. Genuineness may be defined as sincere and honest sharing of oneself. This is not always as simple as it might sound. For example, when confronting one's brother about the self-injurious behavior being observed, it might be very easy to say, "You arc being a real jerk when you do that! Don't you understand how much you are hurting mom and dad!?!" Family know each other in ways no one else can. This is a beautiful quality of this kind of relationship. One of the downfalls of such a relationship is that sometimes such knowledge can affect genuinely sharing something with one another. This example might sound like the brother is genuinely sharing. However, genuineness is diminished because the brother is not sharing about his experience but making a judgment about the behavior. Additionally, he is pointing to others' suffering rather than his own. A more genuine response might be, "When I see those cuts on your leg, I feel really scared and confused. I don't understand but I want to. If you ever want to talk with me about what is happening, I would really appreciate it." This response is hard to argue because it is the individual's experience. How can someone deny what another is feeling? Judgments can be disputed. In this case, the self-injurer can argue that he is not a jerk and his brother always calls him that when he is upset, which derails the attempt at genuineness. The overwhelming amount of research in relationships and communication suggests avoiding judgments, advice, and threats. Family members are encouraged to genuinely describe their experience when confronting self-injury.

Support is also an integral part of addressing self-injurious behavior. It can involve being available emotionally and providing all of the basics of supportive behavior like providing food, clothing, and shelter. However, support does not mean discarding boundaries. Effective boundaries are often difficult in households in which self-injury takes place. One could argue that if appropriate boundaries were in place, the likelihood of this kind of behavior would be significantly decreased. Consequently, boundaries must be practiced. And, in fact, effectively set boundaries can communicate understanding while maintaining one's own sense of self. Much like the concept of genuine sharing, appropriate boundaries are devoid of judgment, name calling, or threats. The ACT model previously described is a good rule of thumb when setting good boundaries. While it was originally intended for children, it can work to some degree with people of any age. When a self-injuring individual becomes distraught because her brother would not loan her his car, a boundary using this model may be useful: "I know you are angry with me for not loaning you my car. But when you don't bring it back when I ask, then I choose not to loan it to you. After I get done using it this afternoon, we can talk about setting up some new rules for borrowing my car." In this example, the brother is empathic. He sets a limit and offers a choice for how they can proceed. It is tempting to discard boundaries when someone is clearly in need of emotional support. However, this example is a supportive method of setting needed boundaries. The individual's feelings are acknowledged. She knows exactly what was not acceptable in the situation and knows how the situation can be corrected.

TAKING THE NEXT STEP

Once the self-injurer has been confronted about her or his behavior, the next step is concerned with how to get help. Help usually will be in the form of an individual, a mental health professional, or a treatment facility. If the self-injurer is an adolescent, parents will often consult with their child's pediatrician. This is a good step for acquiring resources and informing the child's physician of the situation. However, the self-injurer's pediatrician is not equipped to treat the self-injury in that setting. There is no medical solution to the issue of self-injury in the form of a medication or procedure. Certainly, psychopharmacology is frequently a part of a treatment protocol for the self-injurer. In that case, a physician (typically a psychiatrist) is necessary to prescribe medication. But this is only a part of addressing the problem. For someone who habitually uses self-injury, some form of counseling is necessary.

If self-injury is discovered in a school setting, the question of how to proceed will arise. As an understanding of self-injury has improved, means of addressing the behavior, especially in schools, have followed suit. For ethical and legal reasons, schools must typically treat the issue of self-injury as a potential suicide threat. Frequently, after a suicidal ideation assessment, it is discovered that the self-injury is not about suicide but about coping with intolerable affect. However, these issues will likely be treated similarly when first discovered. Next, parents or caregivers will need to be informed. This is where school professionals may have the greatest difficulty. Perhaps a self-injuring student has gathered the courage to share with a teacher, nurse, or school counselor, but she or he does not want the family to know. That school professional cannot promise confidentiality. Parents of a dependent have the right to know about the condition of their child. For the purposes of this section of this chapter, the school professional usually cannot offer the choice of whether parents or caregivers are informed. There are caveats to parents being informed if abuse is indicated. However, this topic is beyond the scope of this chapter. In Chapter 6, a more in-depth discussion will be provided on self-injury in school settings. Since the counselor typically cannot control making contact with parents or caregivers, this can often be a source of intense emotional outbursts on the part of the self-injuring student. Control over life events has been scarce for the student, and now the one thing she or he does control is being threatened. One thing that can be offered to the student is how the school professional and the student can talk with parents and caregivers. Together, they can decide how the self-injury can be revealed. Often, power in some capacity will alleviate the initial threat of talking with parents or caregivers. Of course, there is nothing easy about this prospect. A school professional who is willing to support the self-injuring student emotionally while offering choices on how to approach discussing the problem with parents will likely experience more success in maintaining a relationship with the student while completing his or her ethical and professional duty.

If the individual is an adolescent, parents or caregivers have the right to provide care for their child. Much like the previous example, a self-injuring adolescent may be quite resistant to counseling or treatment. This is a place where concepts like empathy, setting limits, and choice giving (previously discussed in this chapter) can be helpful. While a choice of receiving help may not be an option, choices in where the self-injurer receives help can be. It is important to remember that a vital coping skill is on the verge of being removed from this person's life. This is a threatening prospect. Some power in her or his own destiny may be a better prospect. The following statement may be useful: "I know you are angry with your mother and me for confronting you about cutting yourself. But, we all need help in how to deal with this problem. There seem to be three choices of counselors. Which one of these sounds like the best choice to you?" This is a difficult process regardless of skill in providing support and empathy. Tears, angry outbursts, and dramatic confrontations may still be a part of it. Using these skills may start the family down the path of appropriate expression of support and caring while getting the self-injurer the care she or he needs. Feelings of betrayal and guilt are natural. But, rest assured, outside assistance is necessary and will be the best option for the individual.

If the self-injurer is an adult and is not homicidal, suicidal, or legally found to be incompetent, those who confront the behavior and insist on getting help do not have as much power in the scenario. If the individual is independent, he or she can make his or her own choices and may very well resist the plea to seek help. In this case, the best a concerned individual can do is to decide the terms of how to proceed in the relationship. One could insist that, for the relationship to continue, help must be sought.

It is important to make sure the self-injurer knows that he or she is not the only one being affected. It is common for self-injurers to believe that they do this for themselves and that they are the only ones affected by it. Of course, this is not the case. Friends and family may be worried and distraught over the behavior. Coworkers or supervisors may observe a decline in performance, making their jobs more difficult. Some may choose to limit the amount of contact they have with the self-injuring individual because the behavior is too disturbing for them. Others may feel their own sense of hopelessness and depression about it. In any case, it affects an entire system, and the self-injurer must be made aware.

COMMON DIFFICULTIES IN RESPONDING TO SELF-INJURY
Anger and Fear

Many family members report feelings of anger and fear when learning that a loved one is cutting. These are natural feelings. Perhaps the best route to take in experiencing feelings is to allow oneself to have them. Family members may feel the need to hide their emotions citing that the self-injurer cannot handle them. Consequently, all involved begin to walk around each other and communication is disconnected. Healthy and appropriate communication is appropriate and, in fact, healthy for the self-injurer and her or his family alike. It is important to note that expression of these emotions is often confused with rage toward the client. Rage often will involve name calling, broad judgments, and even intimidation. These are poor methods of self-expression. In any case, a scenario that contains these qualities has a poor chance of ending well. Expression of feeling is appropriate. The self-injurer must learn how to experience feelings without necessarily acting on them. Family members who can express their feelings and not act on them provide a model for appropriate behavior. Beyond that, family members need to take care of themselves too.

Changing how the self-injurer operates more often than not requires the family to function in new ways. Feelings of anger and fear are to be expected. Family members should find ways to express their feelings with a safe individual or through productive and healthy means.

For instance, Shandra is angry with her self-injuring brother, William, because he did not pay back the $20 he owes her. Shandra punches William in the shoulder and stomps out of the house as she proclaims, "I hate you! I can't believe I ever trusted that you would pay me back! You are worthless!" This is certainly an expression of anger. However, everyone involved is harmed in the exchange. William comes away from the experience with his feelings of shame and guilt confirmed. Shandra leaves the experience feeling guilty with how she concluded the confrontation and knowing that she will owe William an amends of some kind.

It makes sense that Shandra is angry with William. If she could have found a way to express her anger with a friend or family member or even write or sketch out her feelings with William, she may have reacted differently. A different way of expressing her anger with William could look like the following: "I am really angry. When I loan you money and you tell me you will pay it back, I expect that you will do it. When you don't pay me back like you said you would, then I choose not to loan you any more money."

In this example, Shandra is clearly angry, but calm with William. She goes on to describe her expectation with him and how she plans to proceed. This statement does not possess any judgment or threat, but a clearly stated boundary that opens up the opportunity for discussion between the siblings. This kind of open dialogue takes time and practice. No one can be expected to express themselves perfectly each time a feeling exists. However, if communication is delivered in a genuine and caring way, the self-injurer will receive practice in and modeling of appropriate expression of feelings. And, just as important, family members will have their needs met as well.

"I Just Can't Look at the Blood or the Scars"

Many family members will describe that looking at fresh cuts or scars is simply too difficult. It is not necessarily important to look at cuts or scars. It is up to the individual whether or not to look at the cuts. It is important to understand the purpose of the cuts or scars being displayed. If the self-injurer asks her or his mother to look at a fresh cut that is still bleeding, the most important step is not looking at the wound but establishing the purpose for showing the wound. The individual may best respond by assessing if the cut needs medical attention, and, if this appears to be the case, secondly, it would be appropriate to establish with the self-injurer the purpose of insisting that the wound be cared for prior to any discussion. This clearly defines that expression of emotion can wait until medical needs are met. If the self-injurer is seeking medical attention for her or his wound, it is completely appropriate to ask a family member to look at it.

If the family member suspects that the display is intended to evoke an emotional response, that family member may ask the question, "What is the purpose of showing me this cut?" The family member can then insist that the cut be cared for. Once medical attention is complete and the wound is managed, the family member can ask that any emotional needs can be discussed rather than making a cut to communicate feelings being experienced.

"If You Would Just Stop Cutting"

Many self-injurers have repeatedly heard how their lives would be improved if they stop cutting. Friends and authority figures will make such statements accompanied by advice on how the self-injurer can actually stop the behavior. This kind of feedback will most likely make no impact on a well-defended exterior or it will serve to contribute to an already abundant reservoir of shame and guilt about the behavior. The self-injurer often simply knows no other way to alleviate stress and self-soothe.

A family member delivering this message can even further exacerbate shame and loneliness. Advice on how to stop self-injuring simply does not work. Furthermore, these statements can be hurtful driving the self-injurer further into oneself. As opposed to advising, the family member would be better served by expressing feelings in an appropriate way. For example, "I am concerned about the cuts on your arms. I imagine you are really in a lot of pain." Or, if the self-injurer is willing to speak about her or his concerns, the family member could simply listen. The self-injurer will likely respond more favorably to empathy and a listening ear than advice.

"Where Should I Hide the Knives?"

Many family members (particularly parents) often will hide sharp objects for fear that the self-injurer will use them to cut. While the intent of the gesture is commendable, likely the effort is wasted. At first glance, it would make sense to hide all of the sharp objects in the house. After all, one would not stock the shelves of an active alcoholic's pantry with alcohol. Unfortunately, no one can stop the self-injurer from completing a self-injurious act if that is her or his intent. To begin, self-injury can be implemented with a variety of devices, surfaces, and textures. Anything from the edge of a piece of paper to a paint chip can be used if cutting instruments are not available.

But, more importantly, if this gesture is made, the self-injurer is informed that she or he is not responsible for managing her or his own emotions. Someone else will do it for the individual. If the self-injurer is truly incapable of regulating her or his emotions without the use of self-injury, more help is needed. Struggling over the behavior in the form of chastisement or shaming is often fruitless. This sort of response will simply promote further discourse in the home and often exacerbate the behavior. Making a plan to get help through a therapist or treatment facility will often provide some relief. Furthermore, empathizing with her experience and avoiding blame for the behavior are in order. Communicating an understanding that cutting serves a purpose and maintaining firm but supportive boundaries will be of better service.

Conclusion

Ultimately, self-injury is incredibly difficult to understand and manage for the self-injurer, friend, and family member alike. Being patient and lowering expectations for all involved are recommended. As has been promoted in this chapter, communication and empathy followed by firm boundaries will better serve the situation over advice and blame.

CHAPTER 5

Treatment and Prevention of Self-Injury

Therapeutic treatment of self-injury (suicidal or nonsuicidal) has been the emphasis of numerous studies. From these studies and numerous case reports, a variety of approaches to working with self-injury have been derived. Unfortunately, along with numerous approaches remains much confusion among the therapeutic community on how best to work with self-injurious behavior.

Much of the literature focuses on better understanding the purpose of the behavior. This is crucial. If the therapeutic intervention provided is not based on this knowledge, little can be gained. This is a prevalent, maladaptive behavior that yields diminishing returns and promotes a great deal of anxiety for those involved. If all involved in the treatment can understand this reasoning, then a myriad of interventions can be fruitful. The purpose of this chapter is to discuss the therapeutic approach to nonsuicidal self-injury as a whole. The following sections of this chapter are designed to provide some insight into some established therapeutic practice, as well as to introduce some basic norms that must be addressed when working with the self-injurious individual.

ASSESSMENT

Prior to the development of the DSM-5 diagnosis, assessment of self-injurious clientele in community agencies, hospitals, and clinical practices might have included diagnosing the individual with borderline personality disorder. With its own diagnostic criteria, nonsuicidal self-injury now can be better assessed by practitioners. Clear and distinct criteria for the behavior itself means new possibilities for study. For the time being, self-injury will still be seen as a secondary diagnosis in most clinical circles. For example, if an individual who self-injures is being treated for chemical dependency or eating disorder, of course one of these conditions will be seen as the primary diagnosis. Self-injury can certainly be addressed. However, symptom relief for one of these respective diagnoses will be the measure of successful treatment. With that said, self-injury will be seen as a concerning behavior by most practitioners. So much of the painstaking research that has been conducted on self-injury has included detailed description of the use and reasoning behind the behavior. While clinical settings may not see self-injury as a primary diagnosis, most will certainly see it as a behavior that must be addressed.

Regardless of diagnosis, practically every clinical setting will assess a client upon entrance into the establishment. Usually this includes an intake process. Client or patient intakes can often be completed by the individual in the form of self-report. Or, if the individual is ultimately not responsible for self-care, then a parent or guardian may complete the intake. As with many diagnosable mental health concerns, there is usually a combination of biopsychosocial factors to consider when assessing the self-injuring individual.

In regard to nonsuicidal self-injury, Barent W. Walsh (2012) has identified these factors as environmental, biological, cognitive, affective, and behavioral. In other words, self-injurious behavior can best be conceptualized if attention is paid to the interrelationships that exist between these factors.

Environmental

To understand the environmental elements of the individual, a detailed description of the individual's family history must be provided that includes family-specific variables that have been observed by the individual but not directly experienced. For example, if an individual would hear regular verbal fights between parents as a child, this would qualify as a component of family life that the individual observed but did not experience personally. These events cannot be taken lightly. Personal messages, philosophies, and self-worth itself can be significantly influenced by that which is observed within the family.

Marsha Linehan (1993), in her book *Cognitive-Behavioral Treatment of Borderline Personality Disorder*, identifies another important variable when looking into environmental influences. According to Linehan, a determination should be made about the invalidating nature of a family system. An invalidating system does not pay heed to a distressed family member's affect. If a child in an invalidating system feels anger and the rest of the family ignores this affect, the individual may (and usually will) exert other methods to gain needed attention. These methods may come in the form of extreme outbursts or rageful behavior. If an individual feels invalidated, simply expressing oneself does not meet the need. This kind of environment leads to the reinforcement of maladaptive behavior. Of course, self-injury among other dysfunctional behaviors can be a result in such an environment.

The individual's personal history must also be taken into account. Personal history includes those events in which the individual has direct and personal experience such as sexual, physical, or emotional abuse. Grief that is associated with a death of a loved one, divorce, or an altered relationship are substantial contributors in conceptualizing the origins and significance of self-injury in a person's life.

A few more words on altered relationships may be in order. Relationships may be completely dissolved. This would stimulate a grief response for a tangible loss. "Altered" means that important relationships remain intact. However, there is a different and often unsettling dimension present. For example, if a parent or guardian suffered a debilitating accident in which the person suffered immobilization caused by paralysis or brain trauma, this could potentially hinder the quality of the relationship. Or, perhaps a parent could suffer from alcoholism, drug addiction, or depression. At the very least, children in such a situation may experience a sense of diminished safety. If the parent is incapable of physically providing security, the child's capacity for emotional expression can become limited.

In addition to past personal and familial experience, the individual's current environment must be examined to determine potentially triggering circumstances. Grieving, experiencing abusive or unhealthy relationships, or other unresolved stressors can all be significant in providing these triggers. If an individual has suffered any of the familial or environmental factors previously described, that individual can experience emotional dysregulation in a variety of scenarios that resemble these past environments. This is perhaps one of the most important reasons for gaining an insightful and factually accurate client intake, including personal and family background, as well as a detailed description of current environment.

Biological

Much of the self-injury literature discusses genetic predisposition. It is important to note that predisposition toward emotional dysregulation is indicated more than a tendency toward self-injury. Self-injury is simply a means through which the affected individual seeks to self-soothe. With that said, self-injury is often sought out to attain this goal. There is little explanation available for how genetic predisposition toward mood states like depression or anxiety may strike any one person. There is also little research that suggests an individual's actions and environmental components do not contribute to mood states. Nevertheless, biological factors must be accounted for.

When discussing biological sensitivity, the unfortunate reality of exposure must be mentioned. Those individuals suffering intrauterine exposure to substances like alcohol and opioids are threatened with the possibility of damage to the brain and central nervous system. An example of such a condition would be fetal alcohol spectrum disorder (FASD). FASD is a result of drinking by the birth mother throughout pregnancy. To date, FASD is the largest known cause of birth defects in the United States. Individuals suffering from this condition can be at a significant disadvantage in physical, cognitive, and emotional development. Damage to structures in the limbic system can occur through intrauterine exposure, as well as environmental stressors leading to trauma. In any case, a poorly equipped limbic system leaves the individual at a disadvantage emotionally and, consequently, cognitively. If emotions are not regulated, the ability to develop memory and learning are inhibited. When conducting a client-patient intake, insight into client exposure, as well as history of family of depression, anxiety, alcoholism, or other conditions, will facilitate a more informed evaluation.

Other biological factors like serotonin system dysfunction and endogenous opioid system dysfunction may also be considered when conducting an intake. The practitioner may look for signs of mood dysfunction like depression and/or anxiety when considering issues with serotonin. As described in Chapter 2, the neurotransmitter serotonin is believed to be greatly responsible for mood regulation.

Opioid system dysfunction involves a diminished experience of pain when performing the act of self-injury. When the individual self-harms, the brain releases opioids. The result is a pleasurable or euphoric sensation. This sensation promotes the continued use of self-harming behavior. As the individual cuts, an analgesic quality is present. This encourages continued self-injury. Conversely, some individuals may experiment with self-injury but not experience the euphoric sensation. Consequently, this individual will likely discontinue the behavior due to the distasteful pain. In habitual use of self-injury, this may serve as an explanation for the individual's apparent insensitivity to pain.

Cognitive, Emotional, and Behavioral

The cognitive, emotional, and behavioral dimensions are closely linked and warrant being mentioned together. A cognitive approach to counseling is quite common in therapeutic treatment. A cognitive therapeutic intervention is based on the premise that dysfunctional thinking and action lead to negative experience of emotions. Dysfunctional thinking ("I can never do things right") combined with ineffective behavior (e.g., avoiding studying for an exam) results in negative affect (e.g., shame, guilt, fear, anger, loneliness). The simple, but not easy, solution to this process involves a change in thinking and action. In this instance, a new thought process ("I can do this by setting measurable and attainable goals") accompanied by a change in behavior (e.g., setting aside a measurable amount of time to study each day) will result in feelings of happiness and contentment. This is an overgeneralization, of course. This therapeutic process can take time and extensive practice. But, in theory, it is a sound basis for change.

For an event to emotionally harm an individual, that person must acknowledge that harm has been committed. It is rare that an individual who has suffered trauma (i.e., abuse) or significant loss (i.e., death of a loved one) does not also participate in at least some maladaptive thinking. A thorough assessment of the self-injuring individual must include the depth and types of thinking and behavior that result in negative reactions to affect. Usually, receptivity to new ways of thinking and action will be integral in developing healthier and more facilitative skills.

As Walsh (2012) indicates, each of these components does not exist in isolation. They operate in relation to one another. An assessment of these variables will assist in developing a treatment plan specifically tailored to the self-injurer. Of course, this is not an easy process. An accurate assessment relies on accurate information. Gleaning information from the self-injuring individual may be fraught with complications. Often the individual does not wish to discontinue self-harming behavior. It serves a purpose. Even with a willing participant, sometimes an understanding of functioning is not accessible until the individual has experienced some therapeutic intervention. Self-awareness may be limited while in the depths of dysfunctional behavior. Consequently, information provided may be sparse or even inaccurate. As insight improves, the individual becomes more capable of providing complete information, and more successful treatment can ensue.

ESTABLISHING A THERAPEUTIC RELATIONSHIP

There is perhaps no more impactful component in recovery from self-harm than the therapeutic relationship. When conducted skillfully and patiently, this relationship can perpetuate immense results. If approached from an uninformed and nonempathic perspective, the therapeutic relationship can have devastating consequences on the recovery process. The therapeutic process is as much an art as a science. While counseling any patient or client should be based on scientifically derived best practices, a certain amount of artful intuition must be present in the practitioner. This quality is usually developed through long experience as a counseling professional but also through working with trauma and affectively challenged clientele.

Carl Rogers (1961), one of the most influential theorists in modern approaches to psychotherapy, identified three components necessary in developing the therapeutic relationship: empathy, unconditional positive regard, and genuineness. Empathy is a quality of relating to an individual. To empathize with someone is to understand that individual's perspective. A common misunderstanding about empathy is that it is synonymous with agreement. This is inaccurate. Empathy simply allows the patient or client to be heard and the listener to understand. Unconditional positive regard means that the individual is supported and accepted regardless of what is said or done. This perspective does not necessarily condone behavior. It actually communicates general respect. And, finally, genuineness refers to being truthful with the individual. In a therapeutic sense, an example of this concept would be confronting the individual if she or he were to share two pieces of information that were not consistent with one another.

For example, Matt, a client of Tara, shares his unconditional love and loyalty to his mother. Later in the session, he shares how much he actually dislikes his mother. Tara, noticing this polarity in thought, replies, "Matt, earlier you said that you loved your mother and now I hear you reporting that you strongly dislike her." This is only one example of a concept that possesses many permutations. While this was the theoretical basis for Rogers's work with his patients, these concepts are considered by many theoretical perspectives as basics in interaction. Their respective stances on change within the patient may be quite different than Rogers's. In any case, there is no wrong theory for working. These are simply theories that have shown therapeutic progress with patients.

Rogers's perspective provided the basis for allowing the professional to therapeutically "hold" the patient. In other words, the patient will need room to roam emotionally and cognitively. She or he may need to be angry and frustrated, lonely and tired, unable to move and unwilling to sit still. The therapist must be able to stay with the patient. This does not require verbalizing the correct phrase or teaching the client how to proceed. Rather, the most therapeutic action might include a willingness to accept the patient as he or she *is* in the moment. This might sound simple, but it actually requires a deep understanding of one's own personal feelings and an understanding of the patient's inevitable projection of feelings and thoughts onto the therapist. In addition, practical experience with self-injury is a must. However, it is essential to understand that the basic therapeutic tenets just described are at the core of any therapeutic alliance that endeavors to move forward.

While it would appear that experience with self-injury should be the primary indicator of successful practice with this population, many practitioners indicate that the behavior simply goes with the territory. It is an understanding of what lies at the core of the behavior that is most important. Some individuals will self-injure, some may be influenced by addiction, and others may suffer with eating disorder. Or, there may be a combination of these behaviors. In many instances, some patients or clients will move to a new behavior. At first glance, if this involves no longer participating in cutting or self-mutilating, the problem would appear to be concluded. However, if the individual has begun to abuse substances or participate in disordered eating habits, has the core issue been resolved? Likely, the answer is *no*. In any case, the seasoned mental health professional should be capable of moving with the client through various behaviors. Any of these behaviors requires in-depth understanding of the respective best practices. This is to say that when identifying a mental health professional to work with the self-injurer, the best question may not be, "Have you worked with self-injury?" The better question might be, "Do you understand why self-injury occurs?"

REPLACING BEHAVIORS

The hope of anyone who cares for the self-injurer would involve adopting new and more functional behaviors. Many parents and caregivers will maintain, "If you will just stop cutting, I know you will feel better." This philosophical approach has resulted in desperate acts like removing sharp objects from the house. Loved ones may propose replacement of self-injury by snapping rubber bands on the wrist or cracking an egg over an area normally reserved for cutting to simulate the sensation of blood dripping. Some have recommended drawing a thick, red line with a magic marker where a cut would regularly occur. In some cases, some parents or caregivers have even threatened restraint. While these may sound like extreme measures, they are usually executed with the best intentions. Initially, it is assumed that the behavior is to blame when, in fact, the behavior is secondary to the internal emotional health of the individual.

This person would not self-mutilate if emotional equilibrium were established. The internal experience of the self-injurer is often an emotional maelstrom. Lack of emotional awareness combined with a maladaptive coping skill that can further separate one from the emotional chaos is a difficult combination to crack. Nevertheless, alternative behaviors are frequently proposed by those close to the self-injurer likely with little to no success.

From a therapeutic perspective, techniques similar to the ones just described should be considered half measures. The consideration of alternative methods can certainly be (and often is) proposed even early in treatment. However, the expectation to cease self-harming behaviors may be considered ambitious at best. The therapeutic alliance must be well in place before most self-injurers think of eliminating the behavior. The individual will usually need to feel as if the therapist has her or his best interests in mind prior to proposing new methods. This takes time and a tremendous level of trust. The response to this statement might be, "Of course the therapist has your best interests in mind!" However, for the self-injurer, the proposition of taking away a valued behavior is likely not considered "best interests." One cannot propose removing something without replacing it with something else. Furthermore, this replacement cannot be a near replication of the self-injury itself. In effect, while the techniques previously described are not harmful, they resemble the behavior that does harm. While the snap of a rubber band will not break the skin, it represents the same method of operation, distraction from intolerable feelings and thoughts. Replacement behaviors must involve new ways of self-expression that do not cause harm or in any way resemble harm to the self, but actually promote self-awareness and self-acceptance.

This is part of the therapeutic process. Moving from an understanding of the motivation to self-harm to a willingness to explore new ways of managing feelings is a difficult process. This takes time and patience from all involved. It must be understood that there will be good days and bad days. On good days, the self-injuring individual may choose more nurturing and sustainable behaviors like journaling, meditation, and diaphragmatic breathing. The individual may choose talking to a close friend about frustrations and disappointments. Exercise and nutrition, for the purpose of maintaining the body as opposed to punishing it, can be implemented. All of these behaviors and more can be available to the self-injurer as alternatives to cutting. First, education about self-injury and its motivations must be gained. Next, the individual must be able to see that these concepts can apply to her or him.

COGNITIVE TREATMENT

Education is an integral part of the treatment of self-injury. Education is a key component in the cognitive approach to counseling in general. There are several schools of thought on the cognitive approach to therapy. However, the basic premise involves changing one's thinking and action to influence emotional and physiological outcomes. Education is not necessarily focused on facts regarding self-injury, although these might come to light. The educational component is aimed at identifying thinking and behavioral processes that assist or hinder the individual in his or her therapeutic process.

One of the first steps in this cognitive therapy process involves identifying and labeling cognitive distortions. In theory, if patterns of thinking can be identified, the individual is better equipped to limit, modify, or altogether change negative thinking processes. In the therapeutic process, the individual will be educated on how to label a variety of cognitive distortions. There is a long list of these maladaptive thinking patterns that include but are not limited to:

- All-or-nothing thinking—characterized by the use of words like *always* and *never.* For example, "I never get what I want."
- Overgeneralization—using limited negative experience to determine that all events will turn out negatively. For example, a young man is not invited to a party. Consequently, he believes that no one would ever want him as a friend.
- Fortune-telling—making negative predictions about upcoming events. For example, "I know I am going to fail my mid-term exam."
- Mind reading—thinking that others believe negative things about oneself. For example, "I can tell just by the way she looked at me that she doesn't like me."

These are only a few, select cognitive distortions that most, including the self-injurer, participate in at one time or another. The more pervasive a condition or diagnosis, the more commonly these distortions will be displayed. A significant amount of energy is spent challenging these maladaptive thoughts by the therapist. This is addressed through a myriad of techniques that may include identifying core negative and positive beliefs. By developing tools to challenge or diminish negative thoughts while accentuating positive ones, the theoretical probability that the individual will feel better about her or his overall self increases. This theoretical perspective is facilitative in several ways. To begin, it is a simple approach.

Table 5.1. Thought and Feeling Log

Event	Thought	Feeling	Feeling Intensity (1 = low, 10 = high)	Alternative Thought or Action
Walked past ex-boyfriend in the grocery store.	He didn't notice me. I want to cut myself.	Pain Anger	9 7	It hurts that we broke up. I can write a letter sharing my thoughts and feelings about our break-up.

Cognitive theorists have worked extensively to develop tangible exercises that include worksheets and activities that are easy to implement by the therapist and the individual alike.

Some examples of exercises include thought logs. A thought log is a means of journaling that involves actively considering the thinking process in regard to events in the day-to-day life of the individual. Table 5.1 provides an example of a thought log.

This form of journaling allows the individual to see potential maladaptive thought processes and potential alternatives to these thoughts. Of course the alternative may or may not be implemented. However, at the very least, a new process can be identified. When completed on a regular basis (as indicated by the empty cells in the example above), the individual can begin to identify patterns in thinking and even observe improvements in thinking.

Other cognitively oriented activities can be practiced that emphasize stress management that does not involve self-harming, tangible activities that can assist the individual in appropriate boundary setting in relationships, and effective communication skills. Perhaps the most appealing quality to the cognitive approach involves simplicity and tangibility of the activities and process. The skills and activities are often designed in such a way that the individual can complete them without substantial instructions. These tangible activities also make for easy collaboration between therapist and patient or client.

The cognitive approach is particularly applicable to this issue because thinking processes almost always present flaws with the self-injurer. This is a therapeutic issue that simply must be addressed. However, changing maladaptive thinking is only one component in the therapeutic process. A limitation in cognitive approaches is that if activities, completion of assignments, and thinking alone are emphasized, it can be easy to de-emphasize the most healing aspect of therapy, the relationship. Sound practitioners of cognitive approaches take this into account and guard against such occurrences. The fact is that facing maladaptive thinking and creating new processes to affect emotional change is an extraordinarily difficult and often grueling process. There will be ups and downs. Typically, the self-injurer will use the behavior again at least once even if new and more facilitative means of functioning are put in place. The solid therapeutic relationship characterized by empathy, unconditional positive regard, and genuineness is designed to withstand these difficult processes and, consequently, always provide support for the individual through the most challenging trials. Regardless of theoretical orientation, this must be valued above all else by the practitioner.

FAMILY THERAPY

Family involvement in recovery from self-injury can be a complicated variable. The call for family therapy may depend upon the individual's ability to maintain boundaries, effectively communicate affect, and cognitively and emotionally remain present in the room. If the individual is unable to complete these three tasks, family therapy would serve little purpose except to trigger the self-injurer. In a case like this, family therapy might be postponed until the individual in question can complete these tasks. These tasks would be addressed through individual or group therapy. As the individual develops a greater sense of maintaining these stated tasks, the usefulness of family work can be better realized.

The individual may also resist the idea of working with the family. A myriad of reasons exist for this resistance. If the individual is an adult and does not intend to seek support and/or an ongoing relationship with family members, family work simply might not occur. The self-injurer may have determined that she or he does not wish to mend these relationships. As an adult, this is the right of the patient or client. Furthermore, the mental health professional must respect this resistance even if it is believed that the individual would benefit greatly from the process. Sometimes, as individual or group therapy progresses, the appeal or benefit of family work can be understood. However, this cannot be pushed. The individual must come to this conclusion in her or his own time.

Otherwise, tremendous effort and attention to therapeutic process may be wasted.

If the patient or client is a minor, family therapy might be a necessary part of the process. In fact, it is rare that some form of family dysfunction does not exist in the case of self-injury. In some cases, sexual, physical, or emotional abuse may have occurred. This will make family therapy exceptionally difficult to complete. The self-injurer would need an assurance of safety. In other words, she or he would need to know that content shared in the session will not be a precursor to further abusive behavior. This is a difficult assumption. No guarantees can be made. If behavioral changes are made on the part of the abusive family member, perhaps significant work can begin. If no changes can or will be made by the abusive family member, it is unimaginable that the self-injurer will be capable or willing to engage in the therapeutic process with the family. If the self-injurer begins to possess a greater and healthier self-concept, why would she or he choose to place her- or himself in harm's way? The environment must be safe and possess the genuine desire for positive change by all involved.

In another instance, the self-injurer may be involved with a family in which there is no abuse. Rather, the individual perceives a broken or damaged relationship within the family. This perception can result from parents or caregivers who are not consistent or even active participants in the relationship. As children learn a great deal of managing emotions from observation of and interaction with caregivers, this circumstance can have a profound impact. Parents or caregivers working exceptionally long hours as a result of a demanding occupation or multiple work shifts may fit into this category. Perhaps a caregiver may suffer from depression, anxiety, alcoholism, or some other mental health diagnosis. In any case, these conditions can contribute to the self-injurer's perception that the caregiver cannot accept or tolerate any relational difficulties that she or he can present.

The paradigm of a damaged system is often a new concept for members of the family including the self-injurer. Often, the self-injurer is seen as the primary problem when, in fact, the system is broken or damaged. If all parts of the system, including the self-injurer, were to develop new methods of coping, communicating, and empathizing, significant advances could occur. This is often the focus of family work. Instead of seeing the self-injuring individual as the focal point for problems with the family, she or he is seen as one part of a greater whole. All the parts must be examined in conjunction with one another. This requires the capacity for self-awareness and vulnerability. All involved must acknowledge their respective part in the process. When this occurs, family therapy can serve as an integral piece in the recovery of the self-injurer. However, it is important to note that the primary focus is not only the well-being of the self-injurer but the well-being of all who participate in the family system.

CONCLUSION

The purpose of this chapter was to provide an overview of the possible directions of therapy for the self-injuring patient. While the components expanded upon in this chapter represent a garden variety in terms of treatment, no therapeutic process will unfold in the same manner. Every individual presents with different therapeutic needs, and consequently, a cookie-cutter approach to treatment simply cannot be expected. The previously mentioned concepts are seen as a guide for what might be expected in a treatment setting. The reader is encouraged to maintain an open mindset as each facility may possess its own method for facilitating change.

PART II

Controversial Issues

CHAPTER 6

Self-Injury in School Settings

Self-injury in school settings is the touchstone for much controversy. The prevalence of the behavior in school settings, as well as how to appropriately address it, has promoted a dichotomy of opinion among school professionals. Professionals from elementary to high school have expressed fear and confusion about self-harming behaviors. Many familiar questions arise: "Is she trying to commit suicide?" "Is self-injurious behavior contagious?" "How should we address self-injury?" "Why would someone want to cut himself?" "Is the self-injurer dangerous?" These and many more questions are frequently asked. One particularly controversial issue in terms of self-injury pertains to treatment. "Should this behavior be treated in school settings or should it be referred to an outpatient setting?" Another difficult issue for school professionals involves the ethical ramifications of the behavior. "Should this behavior be considered as a suicide attempt?" "Is the student a danger to herself?" The purpose of this chapter is to define the scope of the problem in school settings, address some of the more common concerns that self-injury presents for school personnel, and suggest possible methods for counseling self-injuring students. Additionally, ethical implications in approaching self-injury will be explored.

WHY IS SELF-INJURY SO PREVALENT IN SCHOOLS?

There is no definitive reason for the prevalence of self-injury in school settings. At least, it is hard to research how self-injury seems more common in school settings than in the general population. However, there is a clear distinction between the rate of self-injury in the general population and the rate of self-injury among high school students. According to

Juhnke, Granello, and Granello (2011), about 4 percent of the population participate in self-harming behaviors. When examining rates of self-injury in school settings, that rate ranges from 14 percent–25 percent among high school students (Brausch & Gutierrez, 2010). How can this be explained?

Developmentally speaking, school settings are not only an academic learning environment but a social and emotional one as well. From the time children begin kindergarten, the process of observation and reality testing is in place. Middle school is the time when adolescents begin comparing themselves to their peers. This is characteristically the time when adolescents begin to value the opinions and trends of friends over those of their parents. This is a confusing time. Not only are thoughts on music, technology, the opposite sex, and culture (among other things) sought out, but so are attitudes about self-esteem and self-valuing. It is difficult enough to establish a strong sense of self with all things being equal. In other words, believing in oneself and holding fast to one's own values is challenge enough with steady and consistent variables in place like nurturance, values, and a generally safe environment. One can imagine how difficult this process would be if any or all of these variables were not in place.

When considering development of self-esteem in adolescents, it is important to address the question of coping skills. How do students discover these healthy, or sometimes maladaptive, skills? Likely, this occurs in the place where better than one-third of the day is spent: school. In school environments, children experiment with a variety of concepts that often are garnered from fellow classmates. The development of work ethic, confidence in one's ability to accomplish tasks, and managing social norms are all concepts that can be and often are cemented in secondary school environments. Students also can learn less-adaptive skills from fellow students. Self-injury can be one of those maladaptive skills. Students are painfully aware of the activities of others within their personal proximity. As far back as the 1980s, self-harming behavior like cutting, burning, or otherwise self-mutilating would have been considered by many students to be a strange and frightening behavior. Presently, self-injury is a more accepted form of self-expression.

With a greater acceptance and even appreciation for self-harming behaviors among students, the behavior is frequently observed on campuses. A common theory that exists in regard to self-injury and school settings is that of an epidemic or contagion. *Contagion* refers to the apparent spread of the behavior much like a virus. Many school professionals see the behavior in that capacity as it seems to spread among student populations at an often alarming rate. Students observe peers participating in the behavior and experiment for themselves. This can yield various results for those who experiment with the behavior. For some, self-injury may be attempted once or a handful of times with little self-perceived benefit. The individual does not understand the appeal after experimentation. He or she finds that self-mutilating behavior is accompanied by unwanted pain. It may seem gross or messy. The behavior simply does not elicit the same effects it may for those who employ its use on a regular basis.

But, to others who do seek regular self-harming opportunities, the behavior may be the key to managing overwhelming anxieties. The external pain may, in fact, be a welcome alternative to the emotional pain and rage that exist internally. For this individual, the intricacies of self-injury like methods of cutting or damaging the skin along with observing the drip of blood or the welcome sense of physical pain are valued rituals in the making.

Of course, in a school setting, it may be difficult to distinguish between a habitual self-injurer and an experimenter or dabbler. Each of these individuals may present very similarly at first glance. This presents the appearance of an epidemic. Many reports may arise of students who may have cut or self-mutilated. It would be a mistake to assume that all instances of self-injury in a school environment are apparent. In fact, many adolescents (or adults for that matter) conceal their cuts to preserve the right to continue the behavior.

Regardless, all instances of self-injury must be taken seriously and perceived as a threat to the individual. While the possibility of cutting too deeply is possible, most moderate self-injurers do not intend to commit internal injury. Typically, the purpose is superficial or surface with the intent of causing just enough pain to promote distraction from current emotional distress. This presents an enormous challenge for school professionals. "Who is most in need?" If many adolescents present as self-injuring, who can be dismissed as simply experimenting? Of course, the answer is no one can be. School personnel must and will take each case seriously.

WHAT DOES A SELF-INJURING STUDENT LOOK LIKE?

Interestingly, a perceived "look" of self-injury has prevailed over the years since self-injury has been recognized as a genuine concern. Notice the descriptor *perceived*. Many may see two teenagers walking down the hallway. One girl is wearing black clothing. Perhaps she has colored her hair black, red, purple, or even green. She has painted her nails in a dark color as well, and she is wearing a dark T-shirt with a band name or a social statement emblazoned across the chest. As she walks down the hall, she appears annoyed at the onslaught of foot traffic that moves down the hall. The other student, a young man, wears a button-down shirt and stylish jeans. He appears to be quite popular with friends. He stops at lockers of classmates joking and laughing. Clearly, one of these students is the self-injurer. If the guess was the young lady, it is quite possible that would be an incorrect assumption. It could, in fact, be the young man who commits daily self-injury. In traveling a step further, assume a student has many piercings and even tattoos that are hidden by clothing, but, nonetheless, are present. Can the assumption be made that this is a self-injuring student?

The reality is that self-injury can occur across a variety of individuals from various different social status, ages, gender, or even appearances. Many cases of self-injury occur among the students that appear to have everything together. Just like conceptualizing the behavior, it is important to understand what occurs under the surface. It is almost impossible for school professionals or any mental health professional to definitively identify a self-injuring student by appearance alone. Unless either that student reveals her or his behavior, the behavior is directly observed, or suspicious scars appear in a reasonably open location on the body like the arms or legs, no one can point and proclaim, "There is a self-injurer!"

It takes some level of relationship for school professionals to not only identify but also discuss this behavior with the self-injuring student. This presents another confounding fact about self-injury in school settings. There are only so many school professionals to attend to students on an individual basis. How is the behavior to be treated if school professionals have so many other concerns in which to attend?

School Personnel and Treating Self-Injury

Before addressing the issue of treating self-injury within a school setting, "school personnel" must first be defined. This is a broad term. In fact, school personnel can refer to many different roles within the school environment. Of course, elementary, middle, and high schools all have instructors. While an instructor in a school setting will likely not address self-injury in a treatment manner, observations and interactions with self-injuring students cannot be overvalued. Teachers often are entrusted by students with very personal relationships. Teachers and students interact daily, which can encourage a student to develop trust. In fact, it can be argued that faculty members can be the most influential individuals in the life of a student. Teachers often are the first to alert principals, school counselors, or school psychologists of self-injury among the student population.

Other school personnel are often profoundly impactful on students who self-injure. Principals, coaches, nurses, front desk staff, and custodial staff can develop mentor-like relationships with students. The observations and input of these members of the school personnel can be exceptionally valuable not only in establishing concern for students, but also in bridging a trust gap between students and those who can provide much needed assistance.

When it comes to how treatment of the self-injuring student will be administered, perhaps the most influential personnel consist of school counselors and school psychologists. Depending upon the school district, these individuals have varied duties and responsibilities. According to the American School Counselor Association (ASCA) National Model (n.d.), school counselors are responsible first and foremost for academic, career, and social/emotional development of students. This can encompass many tasks designed to accomplish these broad goals.

In many school districts across the United States, the concept of the school counselor conducting psychotherapy with a student in need is often resisted by school administration. With so many duties to complete to ensure the overall well-being of the student population, extensive counseling services to one or even several students can be difficult at best. Many school counselors simply do not possess the time to provide the therapeutic needs of the self-injuring student. Therapy with a self-injurer can take a great deal of time, over months and, sometimes, years. Sessions are usually facilitated weekly and sometimes twice weekly. While counselors can conduct counseling on a limited basis to attend to a student's immediate difficulties, extensive individual counseling is often considered beyond the scope of duties.

The school psychologist operates in a similar role as a school counselor with some different responsibilities. According to the National Association of School Psychologists (NASP, n.d.), the school psychologist contributes as a member of interdisciplinary teams to address needs of at-risk students and to serve the needs of students with disabilities. Another duty of the school psychologist involves communicating results of psychological evaluations to parents, teachers, and others so that they can understand the nature of the student's difficulties and how to better serve the student's needs. Frequently, a school psychologist will be responsible for the well-being of students at many school locations within a district. Consequently, the school psychologist may often experience the same difficulty in managing the needs of a single student as a school counselor.

As the incidence of self-injury increases in school settings, school counselors, psychologists, and social workers are under greater pressure to present a means of managing the behavior in students. In reality, it is likely beyond the scope of one of these school professionals to treat the behavior. These are well-trained and talented professionals who have a great deal to offer their students. However, the issues that accompany the behavior of self-injury require more involvement than practicality will permit.

There are certainly cases of school professionals who have successfully worked with the self-injuring student in individual and group settings alike. Often these reports are accompanied by the knowledge that these individuals are provided with resources specifically tailored to treating a variety of therapeutic issues presented by students. Some of these resources can include established time set aside for meeting students for individual or group counseling in well-equipped, therapeutic counseling rooms. These rooms contain supplies specifically designed to conduct therapeutic interventions like age-appropriate expressive arts materials, literature, and other age-appropriate supplies. Unfortunately, this may be the exception and not the norm in many school districts. If personnel responsible for these kinds of services can be provided the appropriate resources such as time and materials, then certainly appropriate therapeutic treatment can be provided. If meeting with students in a therapeutic capacity is not supported in the school, that school professional cannot be expected to meet the needs of the self-injuring student. Consequently, it is important for school administration to think critically on how these needs will be met and if the school counselor, psychologist, or social worker will be provided the needed tools to complete the task.

Regardless of a school district's decision toward treatment of self-injury, school counselors, psychologists, and social workers can prepare fellow personnel on how to confront the ever-growing issue of self-injury among the student population. In his book, *Treating Self-Injury: A Practical Guide,* Barent Walsh (2012) identifies integral points for training school personnel on how to respond to the self-injuring student. To begin, training about self-injury should be provided for all personnel who could possibly encounter the self-injuring student. This training serves to unify the staff on their general understanding of the behavior and how to guide students effectively. The training should involve assisting staff members in differentiating self-injury from suicidal behavior. Staff should also be trained to understand the different types of self-injury. More severe or major self-injury may require immediate psychiatric or medical attention. Staff should also gain the understanding that body modification such as tattooing or piercing does not necessarily indicate self-injurious behavior. Last, and perhaps most important, school personnel need to be trained in how to appropriately confront the self-injuring student or how to respond should such a student approach that individual. Generally, a dispassionate and respectful demeanor is best for such a situation. Detailed training on the subject can produce a sense of preparedness and calm for the staff, which will of course benefit students.

Preparedness by school personnel can potentially lead to successful treatment. However, it is likely that treatment beyond the school will be necessary. Extended care requires referral to an outside mental health professional. This can be a complicated issue. Each school district has its own policy on referral to outside resources. If not, school administration will need to determine a referral policy that best serves the needs of the student.

ETHICAL AND LEGAL CONSIDERATIONS

Ultimately, the school maintains a responsibility to the student. This includes, first and foremost, the safety of the student. In their book, *Suicide, Self-Injury, and Violence in the Schools,* Juhnke, Granello, and Granello (2011) identify some ethical considerations to account for when addressing the needs of the self-injuring student. To begin, as previously discussed, the school is advised to develop policies that address the referral and management of self-injurious behavior within the school setting. In addition to meeting the requirements of school policy, these policies must also be in compliance with state laws.

In regard to training school personnel, it is advisable to include all school personnel in trainings previously described. Of course, teachers, principals, librarians, nurses, and counselors would be included in these trainings. But other school personnel including administrative staff, cafeteria staff, and any other employees who are in regular contact with students can be an impactful part of a student's support. No one can truly know who a student will seek out for support. Therefore, ethically, all personnel should be equipped with information on how to best address self-injury.

A frequently expressed concern among school personnel pertains to confidentiality. Many school counselors, teachers, and administrative staff feel conflicted when self-injury is revealed and the student pleads for the behavior to be kept secret. It is hard to make a blanket statement about confidentiality. If a student shares that she or he is self-injuring, trust can be delicate, and the prospect of breaking confidentiality threatens that the student will no longer confide her or his difficulties with the staff member. This is a valid concern. However, confidentiality cannot be guaranteed, especially when the self-injury possesses a level of lethality. In other words, while self-injury is frequently not an indication of suicidal intention, assessment of that possibility should not be overlooked. And, of course, parents have the right to know if their child is potentially in some form of danger. So many variables come to the surface when broaching this subject. Generally, confidentiality must be forfeited if the severity of the behavior cannot be determined or if it is determined that the student is a danger to him- or herself. A general line of delineation should be determined by school administration and shared in self-injury training. This will again contribute to the overall sense of confidence and calm of school personnel. Consequently, this will almost always contribute to the best interests of the self-injuring student.

CONCLUSION

Self-injury has been the source of immense confusion and anxiety among school personnel. There are no easy answers in how to address this behavior and its apparent potential as a contagion in school settings. The greatest equalizer in the treatment and management of self-injury in the school is training for all school personnel. School counselors, psychologists, and social workers can develop and facilitate trainings that can inform and equip all school personnel with a plan of action should self-injury be encountered. School professionals in a position to provide this training are advised to align with school administration to determine the best course of action in preparing school personnel and creating a plan for treatment, referral, or assessment.

CHAPTER 7

Self-Injury and Relationships

Perhaps one of the most controversial issues in dealing with self-injury is management of relationships. Or, as some family members and close friends might indicate, the lack of management in relationships is the compelling factor. The literature has expanded exponentially around the internal experience of the self-injurer and how to regulate emotions. However, there is little research on relationship development with this population. In fact, these are not mutually exclusive of one another. Emotional development happens through experience with one's environment. The environment is largely composed of relationships. Developing them and managing them can be challenging for the self-injurer due to his concern with maintaining his own emotional homeostasis simultaneously. Unfortunately, a pattern of the individual managing life through self-injury or throwing himself into relationship is not uncommon. This creates a turbulent back and forth for the individual and those close to him.

Over the years, particularly with the development of the DSM-5, diagnostic criteria around self-injury have been developed. Nonsuicidal self-injury now possesses its own diagnosis. Prior to the DSM-5, self-injury served as one of the diagnostic criteria for borderline personality disorder (BPD). Unfortunately, particularly in the clinical community, self-injury became falsely synonymous with BPD. With these recent changes in the DSM-5, these two very separate conditions are regaining their own diagnostic autonomy. The defining qualities for BPD include intense and unstable relationships, impulsive behavior (often self-injury), difficulty establishing identity, and outbursts of explosive anger and rage.

While self-injury and BPD became almost interchangeable for many in clinical and nonclinical settings, the propensity for one to self-mutilate was only one factor to consider. In fact, self-injury might have been perceived the least concerning behavior for those closely involved with the individual. Consequently, the perception that a person affected with BPD could change any negative behaviors including self-harm was perpetually in doubt by family, friends, and professionals alike. At present, this doubt still exists. It is now known that self-injury is not only associated with borderline personality disorder but other diagnoses as well. But concerns about the self-injurer's ability to effectively and appropriately manage relationships have not wavered.

Self-injury is a means of affective regulation. Feelings that otherwise have no outlet are channeled into a cut or other self-mutilating act. The result is calm or relief from the stressful situation. This process is repeated continuously with similar, if not diminishing, results. This has been mentioned on numerous occasions throughout this text and cannot be overstated. Also, the behavior remains confounding for those close to the individual. A common complaint is the lack of growth emotionally. Self-injury can placate emotional development and, consequently, have a significant, negative impact on intimate relationships.

A complicating variable is that the world can be a trigger. More specifically, relationships can be triggering. Relationships are often the touchstones for self-injurious behavior. A simple glance from a fellow student at school or a lack of greeting from a coworker can set off an intense cognitive and emotional chain reaction. The consequence of such a predicament is often a self-inflicted wound over the possibility of confrontation or rejection.

Many have likely experienced a similar social event. If a classmate offers a stare, perhaps the individual may approach this person and say, "What is going on? I noticed you were staring at me in the hall earlier." If a coworker does not offer a "hello" after passing in the hallway, maybe the individual might approach the coworker at lunch and say, "What was up this morning? I said, 'Hi' and you just walked right past me." Or, the individual might simply assign no real meaning to these events and move on. Or, furthermore, the individual may just make the internal statement "Rude!" and proceed with his or her day. The difference between this individual and the self-injurer is the ability to determine the meaning of this event internally and assign the proper coping skill. Whether that skill is to address the other person, to establish that the event does not require further emotional energy, or to feel angry or hurt, these are all choices that require an internal locus of control emotionally. The habitual self-injurer rarely possesses this ability. Instead of confronting or moving on, self-injury may be used as a means for communicating affect. "I am angry with you; therefore, I will make a particularly deep and long cut."

After one of these events, he or she may experience an impending level of anxiety and may cut to relieve the stress. Meanwhile, there is no resolution to the event. No existing feelings have been expressed, and the individual is left with a sense of her or his own inadequacy and inability to resolve his or her relationship difficulty. Of course, this is in response to a glance in the hallway or lack of greeting from a coworker. Imagine if this process involved an intimate relationship with a significant other like a spouse, parent, or lifelong friend. If one lacked the ability to assign the appropriate amount of emotional response to interactions with those closest to the individual, daily functioning could be exhausting and overwhelming. Self-injury or some form of dissociation from daily events would be necessary.

Part of recovery from self-injury is establishing new coping skills. Importantly, these new skills will focus on interacting with others in a new way. Gradual development of emotional regulation that does not involve harming oneself will be critical. Of course, this often (but not always) begins with a skilled professional who understands self-injury and can develop a genuine and safe environment with the self-injurer. The ensuing development of internal processing and relationship skills takes time and practice. But, by gaining self-awareness and new coping skills, the individual can begin to function in a new way that hopefully does not require self-inflicted pain to manage the situation.

But therapeutic change does not occur in a vacuum, and the individual cannot be expected to make strides by only visiting a therapist one hour each week. More is required. Moving about one's environment will be necessary. In order to do this, the self-injurer must develop the ability to trust in relationships and develop some level of intimacy with those close to him or her.

The development of intimacy is a big step. Intimacy does not necessarily mean a romantic relationship. Intimacy is really synonymous with closeness or trust. Consequently, intimacy can be developed with a close friend, parent, child, or, of course, a partner or spouse. Learning to develop intimacy with those he or she chooses and manage that intimacy with genuineness is the greatest challenge. In fact, this challenging aspect of recovery could help explain the fact that most who attempt recovery from self-injurious behavior will choose the behavior again at least once. What makes connection and intimacy so challenging for the self-injurer? Challenges to intimacy and connectedness, as well as possible means of developing these qualities, will be the focus of this chapter.

A CONNECTED CULTURE

Quite simply, society is more connected than it has been in recorded time. This is a truly miraculous age of technology and nearly instantaneous connection. With modern technology, it takes little time to begin tasks like face-timing, friending, and messaging. There is no need for face-to-face contact unless it is sought out. One can make contact without the actual presence of another person. According to a survey by Pew Internet & American Life Project (2010), 86 percent of Millennials, 61 percent of Baby Boomers, 47 percent of Generation Xers, and 26 percent of senior citizens reported using social media. We cannot claim that technology is only for the young. Clearly, statistics tell us differently. And when current Millennials are in their 80s, imagine the forms that digital connection will take.

Communication is more convenient and diverse. If an important message must be delivered, there is no need for face-to-face interaction. A text will serve the purpose. Also, with social media outlets, one can get a message out expeditiously. Changing one's status from single to engaged, passing final exams, the acquisition of a new puppy—all of these messages and more can be delivered to the world within seconds. Where multiple repetitions of a letter or phone would have been necessary a couple of decades ago, anything can be mass communicated by almost anyone at any time. And finally, it is now more likely that someone will find a date through the Internet than through connections like work, friends, or religious affiliation. Make no mistake, culture has been improved by these advances. This is a great time!

However, it is also a confusing time. There exist some challenges for anyone in a technologically rich culture. For example, smartphone technology has enabled a person to see people on her or his phone in the immediate area who are interested in meeting. A simple swipe of the finger across the face of the device and in minutes two people are connected. One might say it is the equivalent of a blind date. However, it possesses some differences. A blind date required some relational connection to friends or family who believed this person would be the perfect match (even if he or she wasn't). If one didn't know the date, at least one knew the people who referred the date. That is no longer necessary. Likes and dislikes can be completely anonymous. One can know someone before ever really *knowing* him or her. Arguably this may not be a bad thing. Who wouldn't want to know everything they can about the person they are about to go out with? However, a great deal of emphasis is placed on finding someone and not necessarily knowing what to do once that person has been found. "All of our vitals seem to match nicely online. Now what?" Of course, this is an overdramatization for most. For most people, this process can work out well if the individual possesses the emotional maturity to facilitate the relationship once it is gained. This is not the case for everyone.

As a case in point, how many examples exist of someone firing an angry or enraged e-mail, text, or other digital media to another? Usually this is in response to perceived indignation or humiliation. How often is this done in haste? And, would the same individual make the same gesture if the person at the center of the angst was directly in front of him or her? In many instances, the answer might be yes. However, examples abound of a hasty e-mail being sent and later being regretted due to the harshness and/or inappropriateness of the content.

Furthermore, bullying has taken an unfortunate step thanks, in part, to social media. Bullying has been a problem in school and work environments since bricks and mortar were first laid. The humiliation and subsequent trauma of individuals degrading fellow students or coworkers have been studied for some time now. Research can confirm that bullying has been and is currently a truly traumatic experience for those serving as targets. These already overwhelming events could remain known by only the immediate participants. However, with the emergence of social media, these events may be known by the world. Cyberbullying, or bullying through electronic communication technology, is a growing problem among youth and adults alike. Many accounts of displayed text and photos appear to have ushered in new opportunities for social anxiety. Mistakes and missteps now can outlive short-term memory and be encased literally forever and accessible by anyone.

How do these examples relate to the self-injuring individual? It would be easy to note that these kinds of unfortunate events are the source of self-harm by those afflicted. And, in fact, that may very well be the case. However, these examples are not mentioned because they promote self-injurious behavior. Rather, these are examples of emotional dysregulation within relationship on display.

In terms of the enraged e-mail example, it is a distinct skill to formulate a well-thought-out e-mail or text with perfectly worded contempt for another, insult, or simply unveiling intense anger. It is another skill, or set of skills, altogether to make the same gesture in person with the object of disdain merely feet away from the individual. Furthermore, it is yet another set of skills to deliver the message in person and then be willing to receive that individual's response. And, lastly, it is even more difficult to complete the aforementioned tasks and then actually hear the response of another and take responsibility for whatever consequences may come from the exchange.

It takes practice to be present in a live interaction. For example, Sally and Carlos are in an argument. In the heat of the moment, Sally says, "I hate you and I don't want to see you again." Carlos immediately responds with jaw-dropping silence at what he has just heard. He was not expecting this. His eyes begin to moisten, his lip quivers, and his knees become so weak that he must sit. Sally also was not expecting Carlos's response. She expected him to continue the argument and perhaps return the sentiment. But he didn't. His response was that of pain and sadness.

In a face-to-face exchange like this, Sally must make a choice to take responsibility for her words and actions or remain guarded and shut off from her emotional experience. She may stand by her words, "I really do not care for you and I want you to leave now." She might realize that her words delivered a blow that she never intended prompting her to apologize and state, "I didn't really mean that. I was just so angry with you that I did not know what else to say. I apologize. I don't hate you. I just hate when you do that." Sally and Carlos can now have a discussion rather than an argument. Perhaps they remain friends or maybe they split ways. In any case, this is an example of Sally taking responsibility for her emotions and then of her actions. This is advanced relationship skills in action. This kind of exchange would often be too much for the self-injuring individual (and at times for any of us). Putting words to genuine affect and then exerting willingness to communicate that affect would be a challenge in any environment.

Unfortunately, this kind of conundrum is regularly played out in a social media context. The previous argument might very well occur in a texting exchange. If that were the case, Sally would not have seen Carlos's reaction to her words. Perhaps she would misinterpret his stunned silence for ambivalence to her statement. This could have disastrous results for the relationship.

In terms of self-injury, social media can leave the individual at a disadvantage. Clearly, social media cannot take away the opportunity for genuine, face-to-face contact. People are responsible for those choices. But, if the individual were already at a disadvantage in understanding his or her internal emotional process and consequently taking responsibility for those emotions before action, social media are not designed to assist the individual in developing those much-needed skills. These skills involve first identifying affect, then self-censoring a response to a stimulus, and finally, upon responding, taking responsibility for one's response. Social media has achieved its purpose if the basic message is delivered. Unfortunately, this is insufficient for solid relational contact. As a case in point, two separate texts are sent. Each looks exactly the same: "Look at the road ahead." Is the message that the individual should pay attention to the road that lies before her or him? Or, should he or she be aware that there is a spherical shape in the road like that of a human head? Certainly the second example is a little macabre. However, one can understand the point. Social media often does not communicate affect or intention, but merely fact. There are elements to the message that may be missing unless delivery is very exact. Even then, one cannot account for possible mistakes in the recipient's perception.

GENUINE CONTACT

In a way, social media can act as a diversion to internal process. If the individual experiences confusion around a digital exchange with an online friend, it would be difficult to establish where the difficulty occurred. Furthermore, social media outlets hardly insist that the individual be emotionally available in the moment. Similar to e-mailing a nasty message to a fellow coworker, there is no immediacy. The enraged individual can carefully construct the message before sending. If there is a response, heated or otherwise, the individual can craft another message. Face-to-face contact is different and requires a sense of vulnerability that social media resources seem to lack. In other words, thinking on one's feet in a debate or discussion in a face-to-face interaction is quite different than carefully constructing a response through digital messaging.

Certainly, digital contact is better than none. For self-injurers, there are social media chat rooms and blogs that serve an invaluable purpose. Practice in identifying emotions and then reporting them to another in one's own time can be excellent practice. The danger is in not taking the next step to more genuine contact. When should someone step out to make contact with another? Only that individual will know when he or she is ready. Social media does not stop the individual but offers a distraction.

What is meant by contact? If one were to place her or his hands against a textured wall, that individual has made contact with the wall. As the individual's hands move across its surface, a variety of tactile sensation can be experienced. The ridges and points of a stucco finish, the coolness of fresh paint that has recently been applied, or even noticing the unevenness of the surface are all examples of making contact with the wall.

Now imagine that the same individual were to place his or her hands approximately one inch from the surface of the wall without actually touching it. Is the individual making contact? Not with the wall. Of course, the argument can be made that he is making contact with something (i.e., the air). Now add some distraction to the background. A party with plenty of talking, laughing, and interaction could be a strong distraction from making contact with a wall that is not even being touched. But, nevertheless, the individual is asked, "what does the wall feel like?" What quality of answer can the individual provide? If he or she is not touching the wall and has a great deal of distraction occurring in the background, it will be difficult to truly know the qualities of the wall. Perhaps this is a farfetched example, but it is an apt analogy for the experience of the self-injurer. How can the self-injurer make contact with her or his experience (e.g., feelings, thoughts, how to make a decision) if she or he has distraction? Whether that distraction is actually cutting or checking in with a website instead of conversing with the friend that is sitting next to him or her, opportunity to disconnect from one's experience is all too available. The challenge is making direct contact when distraction is constantly available.

Before condemning the self-injurer for her or his inability or unwillingness to make contact with the experience, it is important to exercise some empathy. Answer the question, "How self-injurious am I?" Perhaps this is a difficult question to answer. Another way of asking the question might be, "How do I limit my contact with my own internal experience and my relationships?" If part of the problem is how the self-injurer handles internal emotions and external relationships (often simultaneously), where did the individual learn those skills? To what degree are substances, food, sex, and relationships part of the individual's system? As a loved one, to what degree are they part of your system? Imagine removing coffee from the daily commute to work or the trip to the fast food restaurant even when you have recently eaten a meal. It is not easy to imagine removing these things from daily existence. Furthermore, if you can remove them, do you miss them? These questions are examples of contact with one's own experience. If one can admit to experiencing difficulty in altering or even removing those things that assist in disconnecting from personal experience and relationships, how can that individual tell the self-injurer, "Stop it"? Simply stopping is usually not an option. Something must be introduced before something can be removed. This is a process for everyone. For the self-injurer, it can be particularly difficult especially if trauma is part of the equation. Connecting to one's true experience of internal process while also connecting in relationships takes an enormous amount of energy, courage, and diligence. It simply takes time and experience in a safe environment that is patient and acknowledging of sometimes slow but nonetheless incremental changes.

MAKING CONNECTIONS

If the primary problem for the self-injurer is managing emotions without cutting while also interacting responsibly within relationships, there must be a solution that addresses these issues. There are a variety of therapeutic interventions that can be implemented to address each of these issues. Explaining the intricacies of these approaches is not necessary for this text. However, it is important to identify good therapeutic processes and what makes them facilitative. It is also important to mention that any of the processes in this chapter do not occur as if one were flipping a light switch. Change is difficult, and it is not always desired, especially by the self-injurer. As with any transformation, the individual must see the benefit of it. If cutting serves as one's respite and security, there is little reason to stop the behavior. Sometimes the individual no longer benefits from the process of physically wounding. Other times, the person must be confronted about her or his choices and their respective effects on self, family, and future. With this said, it is important to note that activities and processes are merely tools for change and discovery. A personal decision and subsequent commitment are necessary before substantial change can occur.

An integral connection for the self-injurer is the one within self. Before one can be emotionally present and responsible in relationship, she or he must first identify his or her own internal process. This process begins with labeling affect and thoughts. It is only logical that someone who has learned to avoid feelings is desperately in need of identifying them. As previously stated, this takes willingness and practice.

One therapeutic process that can serve the self-injurer well is that of journaling. Journaling or writing out experiences and those thoughts and feelings that accompany them has yielded valuable results. What makes this such a useful activity? To begin, writing about experience transports thoughts and feelings from within the mind to the page. By committing to the page, the individual has committed to the thought and feeling. If it is on paper or computer screen, there is no denying that it exists. By observing what has been written, feelings and thoughts come to the surface. If a high school student, Carol, were to describe cheating on her English test, she might define feelings that have developed as a result of her actions: guilt in regard to choosing such an action, shame about not understanding the material, and anger at her instructor for not being more available to her. These are all examples of feelings and thoughts that might be explored. As Carol scans the page of several entries she has made, perhaps she begins to notice themes in her thinking and feeling. She might even be able to tangibly see what prompts her to self-injure. At the very least, she begins to identify with herself. Where previously thoughts might race and feelings are cut away, she can now look at the page and develop a better understanding of herself.

Of course, any kind of writing can be useful. However, specifically writing about events and subsequent thoughts and feelings can be particularly helpful. By following such a model, steps are taken to ensure that writing is not misused. Rather than processing daily events and their corresponding thoughts and feelings, a journal can be used as an instrument to promote self-loathing. If the journal exercise were used to write self-defeating statements like "I am stupid and unlovable" or "I hate everyone! Mainly myself!", greater harm than good can occur. This is not an activity designed to lash out at oneself, but to better understand personal development in the form of affect and thought.

This form of journaling keeps the individual honest about her or his boundaries in the events. Boundaries assist any individual to identify where one person ends and the other begins. If the instructor of Carol's English class, Mr. Williams, were not available to help Carol with the class, that constitutes his part in the event. Carol's part involves her thoughts and feelings about the event and even her behaviors. For example, did she ever ask Mr. Williams for help? If so, and he was simply not available to her, anger and frustration with Mr. Williams would certainly fit. However, if Carol was angry with Mr. Williams and yet she never solicited his help, what is Carol's part in the event now? Perhaps she discovered anger and frustration with herself. Or, she identified fear about asking Mr. Williams for his assistance that then leads to shame about reaching out for help. These feelings are merely speculation on the part of the writer. Carol's feelings may vary greatly from these examples. There is no chastisement for her feelings regardless of how illogical they may seem to others. This is another benefit in journaling. In this example, Carol owns her feelings. They are hers. In any case, if this can take place without Carol being triggered to self-injure, a tremendous advancement has occurred. Furthermore, progress has also occurred if Carol is able to produce an intervening thought prior to self-harming. If a feeling arises and Carol can ponder, "What is going on with me right now?" and she still self-injures, there is still celebration to be had. Carol now has the benefit of self-awareness. She is beginning to delve into her motivation to dissociate from her experience. She has begun the process of identifying her internal struggles. The leap from asking these important questions to pulling out her journal whenever she has a feeling and bypassing self-injury altogether may take additional time and effort. In fact, it certainly will. But the walk of a thousand miles begins with one footstep.

Other forms of writing can be useful as well. Karen Conterio and Wendy Lader (1998), in their book *Bodily Harm: The Breakthrough Healing Program for Self-Injurers*, identify 15 different writing assignments that are designed to assist the self-injurer in organizing thoughts and focusing attention in a manner that is constructive. These assignments range anywhere from an autobiography to identifying "the person I want to be." For many who employ the behavior, self-injury has long served as a means of deflecting or buffering feelings. If feelings are not realized, thinking is not clear. This only contributes to the impulsive quality of self-injury. Writing helps the individual connect to one's experience and get to know her- or himself in a safe environment. While writing is an individual process, it is a good training ground for social interaction. If the self-injurer can begin to identify his or her experience in writing and tolerate the feelings that accompany that experience, firm ground has been laid for the path to responsible relationships.

Connection to supportive environments is also critical for the self-injurer. It is important to note that individuals who self-injure come in many forms. Much of the literature will portray the self-injurer as someone who cannot articulate her experience and is so immobilized by unrealized emotions that she cannot interact with the outside world. Sometimes, this may be the case, but there are many who use self-injury who present quite well. Even if the individual appears to have absolutely no reason for committing self-harm, she has her reasons. She appears to be well adjusted and capable of making her own connections without anyone's assistance.

Regardless of how self-injurers present themselves, they need support like anyone would. The question is not how the self-injurer presents, but what is happening with that individual when she or he is interacting with others. Sarah, a 14-year-old freshman in high school, explains, "I am great with people. My teachers love me. I talk with friends all day. In fact, I am the one most of my girlfriends come to for support. If only they knew that sometimes while I am in a group of total strangers or my best friends, I find myself drifting away. I want to cover my eyes so no one will make eye contact. I imagine wearing this dark cloak so that I can see others, but they can only see my shape. They cannot see my face. Wouldn't it be great if I could pull this off? By the time I am finally alone, all I can think to do is get to my bag, find my makeup kit with my razor, and cut. Then I can do it all over again." By looking at Sarah, no one would ever guess that she self-injures. She is, in fact, a very smart, autonomous young woman. She simply uses physical harm to replace internal, emotional discomfort. Sarah would likely benefit from the activities previously described. She will also benefit from a support system that understands her and is willing to accept her no matter how much her actions or thoughts might be disturbing.

Sarah lacks the tolerance for the difficulties an intimate relationship can present. A friend who is experiencing intense emotions can no doubt trigger Sarah's feelings. Since these are intolerable but she also wants to support her friend, she may just shut down that feeling part of herself until she can isolate and cut to experience relief.

Supportive environments will include family, friends, or caregivers that are willing to express appropriate limits and take responsibility for their own feelings. For example, if Sarah's mother were to discover that she self-injures, it would be natural for her mother to experience concern. For her mother to forbid Sarah from ever cutting again or to ask in a judging tone "Why do you do that to yourself?" would only reinforce Sarah's sense of shame about her behavior. Sarah would likely see her mother as unapproachable about her problems or concerns. These kinds of responses serve to reinforce what the self-injurer already believes, "There is something wrong with me."

A more appropriate response from Sarah's mother might look like the following: "Sarah, I know you cut yourself because you are having a lot of feelings that you need an outlet for. I am certainly concerned, but I know this can't stop all at once. But I do want you to know that I am here for you and I can take any problems that you might present to me. I want to do something to help us out with this. What do you think about that?" In this instant, it cannot be overstated that Sarah needs to know that her mother can handle whatever emotional turmoil Sarah can dish out. Sarah is not presented with ultimatums but sincere concern. Her mother presents her with an opportunity to discuss the issue. The difficult part of this process for the concerned family or friend is that support can be presented and the self-injurer can still shut down. In most instances, self-injurers need time to gain awareness of their own experience. They will also need plenty of practice with tolerance of their own feelings and thoughts before they can be comfortable with intimate relationships. But appropriate expression of concern and setting boundaries that care for all involved can be there for the self-injurer when she or he is ready. In other words, if appropriate expression does not seem to be working, it will not help the situation to become enraged at the self-injurer's lack of response. This will only serve to drive a wedge between him or her and those that can serve as support. Patience and getting the individual the help she or he needs to discover her- or himself might be in order before strides can be made within the relationship. With this in mind, it is always indicated that those members of the support team can seek out their own support and be aware of their own internal experience.

MINDFULNESS

Mindfulness refers to one's ability to attend to the present moment calmly and without emotion. An individual is being mindful when he or she is able to completely engage in the immediate experience without exercising any form of emotional or cognitive dissociation. At any given time, this process can be a challenge for anyone, but it is particularly difficult for the self-injurer.

While this is a reasonably new modality in the therapeutic community, the concept of mindfulness has been at the center of meditative practices like yoga for centuries. Mindfulness practices have been used in a variety of settings with a myriad of populations including, but not limited to, sufferers of posttraumatic stress disorder (PTSD), eating disorder, personality disorder, anxiety, and depression. Mindfulness practices have also been used with athletes, members of the clergy, and academia to name a few. From this short list, it is easy to see that people from all kinds of backgrounds and emotional states may benefit from this discipline. It has proven useful in slowing or even stopping impulsive thoughts and actions, promoting greater intrapersonal clarity, and contributing to improved response to emotionally charged scenarios. The argument can be made that anyone could benefit from mindfulness training.

A primary goal for the self-injuring individual is to gain a sense of emotional regulation without self-mutilating. Another goal is to better manage relationships. For relationships to realize optimal success, both members must possess the ability to be present. Partners must be able to hear, empathize, and appropriately respond to input from one another. This is different from being defended against the content that one's partner can present and having a sound argument for his or her perspective. Being present requires that one listens to what is being presented and processes it without having to discard it, ignore it, or defend against it. This is exactly where the self-injurer can experience difficulty. This is also where mindfulness can produce results.

The practice of yoga can serve as an example of how mindfulness works. Yoga is a discipline that involves the body, mind, and spirit. When yoga originated is a well-debated topic. Some experts reference its origin as early as 2600 BC. Hindu and Buddhist philosophical systems of yoga emerged between 200 BC and 500 AD. In the mid-nineteenth century, it was introduced to Western culture. A more in-depth study of yoga is recommended for those interested in its philosophical teachings. This level of depth is beyond the scope of this text. For a practical example, yoga may be further defined as a series of exercises and postures that are designed to promote a sense of well-being and centeredness. It has also been identified as an excellent form of general exercise with numerous physical and emotional benefits.

How can the mindful practice of yoga prove useful in promoting emotional regulation and, consequently, relationship skills? Assume, for a moment, two exercise scenarios: one, a traditional workout room with weights and various other forms of exercise equipment; and, two, a sparsely populated room with a plate glass window looking upon a wooden background. On the wooden floor of this room is a yoga mat to provide cushion when performing various postures and exercises. A trainer or mentor is present in each of these respective environments. This individual is present to maintain that various exercises and postures are performed correctly and also to provide support, safety, and encouragement.

In the traditional exercise room, imagine an individual going through a workout that includes weight lifting and aerobic exercises. The trainer is present to spot for the individual and to push her to perform just beyond her comfort level. When the individual who is working out approaches 8 repetitions, she is encouraged to push to 12 reps even though she is beginning to lose endurance. She starts on the ninth rep, when she can only push about half way through. The trainer belts out, "Come on! You can do it! Push through! Come on! Don't stop!" The individual finds this motivating. She does, in fact, push through to 10 reps, which is almost to the goal of 12. The trainer congratulates her, and she feels a sense of accomplishment, but perhaps a sense of intimidation. "Can I put myself through this each time?," she questions.

Now, imagine the yoga environment. The individual is in a warrior pose. The warrior pose might be described as a lunge position with arms extended. Throughout the pose, the individual is encouraged by the mentor: "Be present in the moment. If you cannot maintain the posture, amend the posture so that you can keep your body aligned. If you cannot maintain the posture, it is okay to forgive yourself and assume a safe posture." The individual is encouraged and nurtured through the process. All the while, she is learning how to handle the often difficult postures and exercises while also permitting herself the grace of imperfection.

Each of these forms of exercise is beneficial and possess its respective merits. At times, the individual can call upon what she has learned in the weight room. She can push through. She can handle it when she has to do so. Perhaps this can serve as a representation of knowing one can handle an emergency. She may not want to exist in this state on a regular basis, but if it must be called upon, she is up for the challenge.

Now imagine the yoga room. There exist at times uncomfortable postures. Contortions that may be stressful can be maintained as well. There is an equal sense of self-assuredness, a sense that this too can be handled. However, in this environment, there is also a presence of forgiveness if postures are not maintained perfectly. If the individual cannot maintain as indicated, how can she or he amend the posture so that exertion is beneficial and safe rather than calling upon one's shame to push through the exercise?

Could these two exercise scenarios serve as analogies for the self-injurer? Sometimes it is necessary to be in a state of stress and push through no matter what the cost. If the individual must dissociate from the experience to complete the task at hand, so be it. This is a representation of emergency, integration of the brain stem, which is responsible for the fight-or-flight response. Every human has this capacity at his or her disposal. But does the individual need to exist in this state at all times? Almost anyone would exclaim, "Of course not!" However, the self-injurer likely exists in this state for a disproportionate amount of time throughout life.

Could the yoga example serve as an example of how the individual's experience could be? There still exists a need to operate with some stress being exerted upon the body, mind, and spirit. However, there is a voice promoting nurturance. Forgiveness is present if things cannot be maintained exactly as imagined. Mindfulness is the voice shifting from the mentor to the individual him- or herself—an internal voice that provides an internal locus of control. If the individual can begin to operate from this perspective, he or she is developing her or his own internal voice that encourages self-acceptance and forgiveness. This is not an easy transition. The self-injurer often operates from the external voice of someone passing down judgment and loathing. The challenge is to exercise the ability and the willingness to hear the internal voice of support.

Practically speaking, is yoga the answer? For some, it absolutely is. For others, they must find their own discipline. It can be meditatively focusing on a candle or a fixed object. It can be going to a weight room or some other form of exercise. Perhaps it is woodworking, yard work, or practicing a musical instrument. The discipline is not important, but *a* discipline is. Some form of discipline requires the individual to accept the realities that come along with the medium. To acquire a level of proficiency, there must be practice. When a level of proficiency is attained, in the midst of the discipline of choice, the individual can learn to accept that reality as it is at that moment. If the discipline is mowing a yard, the individual will likely not wish for the far corner of the yard to suddenly be manicured but will realize that one can only focus on the strip of grass that is directly in front of the mower. The far corner of the yard will be cared for in time.

Mindfulness can provide a sense of peace and patience with oneself that can be emulated in other parts of life like relationships. Like any of the disciplines mentioned, this is a practice, not a destination. These principles must be put in motion on a regular basis for the benefits to be realized. This is the challenging component. The self-injurer will need support that provides an equal amount of patience and nurturance with firm but appropriate boundaries from loved ones and him- or herself alike.

Conclusion

Intimate relationships provide a challenge for anyone who embarks upon them regardless of one's level of emotional health. The self-injurer will need to develop skills that promote self-regulation while also maintaining the needs of the intimate relationship. As this chapter has indicated, this does not happen in a vacuum. To begin, the self-injurer will need to practice in manageable environments like those provided through therapy or a supportive living situation. As she or he develops enhanced skills in self-introspection, self-acceptance, and self-expression, the self-injurer will develop self-regulation. This will only enhance the maintenance of intimate relationships, which are crucial in the developmental process.

CHAPTER 8

Self-Injury and Group Counseling

Self-harming behaviors like self-injury, eating disorders, and chemical dependency and abuse are complex conditions that often require some form of treatment to relieve symptoms and manage associated, maladaptive behaviors. There are a variety of ways to address these conditions. Twelve-step meetings have been an integral portion of recovery for millions of people since the mid-1930s. In fact, Self-Mutilators Anonymous has recently become available to those who wish to stop using self-injury. Meetings are face to face in some areas but are also offered in an online format.

Of course, there are many self-help texts and materials available on the market for the self-injurer. Since the mid-1990s, many books aimed at those suffering from self-injury, their families, and the therapeutic community tasked with helping have emerged. There are more quality books, workbooks, and autobiographical accounts available than can be listed in this text. A quick search on a major search engine will yield a bounty of resources.

However, as great as these resources can be, more involved assistance is often needed. This can often be in the form of individual counseling or group counseling. Individual counseling is a common recommendation. An individual counselor well-versed in working with self-injury can serve as an invaluable resource for the individual and family alike. It is always advised to research the professional in question. To begin, it is important to realize there are different disciplines of professionals who can be of service. Psychiatrists, licensed professional counselors (LPCs), licensed psychologists, and licensed clinical social workers (LCSWs) with their respective licenses are in a position to provide therapeutic services. A more detailed description of mental health professionals will be provided in Chapter 9.

Groups are also a medium for providing counseling services to the self-injuring individual. Face-to-face groups are often the primary medium for delivery of services in treatment settings. A variety of reasons contribute to this reality. Financially, this medium makes sense for insurance companies providing the funding for treatment options. Logistically, groups often work better for facilities. More patients can be treated at one time. Therapeutically speaking, when treating issues like chemical dependency, eating disorders, mood disorders like depression or anxiety, and self-injury, group treatment can be arguably the most facilitative method of treatment. This chapter will discuss the group process, the drawbacks of groups, and, of course, the benefit groups can provide. The chapter will conclude with a case example of a recovering self-injurer participating in a group.

How Do Groups Work?

Group counseling may be defined as two or more people (not including the facilitator) who meet on a regular basis with the intention of working on intrapersonal and interpersonal concerns. Typically members of a group meet with similar goals in mind (e.g., depression, self-injury, anger management). Counseling or psychotherapeutic groups are led, or facilitated, by a trained facilitator. Therapeutic groups may vary in size. However, the literature suggests an ideal group size would be no fewer than five and no more than eight. Of course, depending upon the environment, groups may fluctuate and ideal size may be impossible to maintain. Fortunately, a skilled facilitator typically can make a group of any size work.

Different than therapeutic groups, self-help groups may be peer-lead. For example, in 12-step circles, this may be a member or trusted servant of the group. In other forms of self-help groups, this also may be a member of the group or someone who possesses a level of knowledge or expertise but is not necessarily a trained group facilitator. While self-help groups are very different in how they are facilitated and they are not considered therapeutic groups, that does not mean that they are not therapeutic. In other words, the individual attending a self-help group may gain an ineffable amount of support, knowledge, and self-understanding from a self-help or support groups setting.

At first glance, it is easy to see groups as a meeting of people who take direction from a group leader or simply chat with one another. However, a well-facilitated group is far more complicated in how it impacts its members. Vinogradov and Yalom (1989) point out that in group therapy, both patient-therapist and patient-patient interactions contribute to the benefit of the participants. Both of these types of interactions are used to promote change in the maladaptive behaviors of each of the group members. The group itself is used as a therapeutic tool, along with specific techniques or interventions used by the trained facilitator.

Groups may be conducted in two very different settings: inpatient and outpatient. Inpatient settings are often referred to as residential treatment programs. Typically, this form of therapeutic intervention lasts at least 30 days. These types of facilities meet daily with patients and employ group psychotherapy as a part of treatment. Inpatient settings are composed of individuals with acute psychiatric problems. For example, an individual checked into a treatment facility with a substance use disorder may also be struggling with clinical depression or an eating disorder. Along with this, the individual may use self-injury to manage intolerable affect. In other words, the patient may be managing multiple issues in addition to the primary diagnosis. These facilities offer safe and structured environments that remove patients from stressful settings that fuel the urge to commit self-harming acts like self-injury, alcohol abuse, or dysfunctional eating. This is often the crucial element that makes the inpatient setting the most appropriate choice for the patient, a change in environment.

Outpatient groups are typically composed of members who are in a more stable level of functioning than their inpatient counterparts. Groups conducted in these settings are often referred to as counseling groups as opposed to psychotherapy groups. These groups usually meet once or perhaps twice each week. It is important to note that intensive outpatient settings are also in existence. In this case, group members meet each day but do not stay in a facility. Intensive outpatient programs attempt to provide many of the qualities of an inpatient setting while providing patients the freedom to maintain commitments to family, work, and educational responsibilities.

Before discussing identified curative factors of groups, a few words must be said about theory in the practice of the group and the self-injuring client. While many studies have been conducted about group interventions used with the self-injuring population, research has failed to identify one approach that appears to work better than another. However, some group interventions seem to come to the forefront. These are in no particular order and it is recognized that other valid and beneficial interventions exist. Cognitive behavioral therapy and dialectical behavior therapy appear to have the most consistent research on positive outcomes of group work with self-injury and coexisting conditions. This statement is not intended to solely endorse these interventions. At the time of this publication, these simply appear to be the two most researched group interventions. With that said, other interventions and approaches are appearing on the scene. Emotion regulation-focused groups, family-based interventions, and expressive arts groups are theoretical approaches that have recently yielded positive outcome research on their respective methodology. Interventions are important. New research comes forward in the therapeutic world that can revolutionize how practitioners assist their patients and clientele. When using group methods to impact self-injurious behavior, or any diagnosis or condition for that matter, group process is perhaps the most imperative variable. Creating a safe environment in which group members can develop relationship and receive support mixed with therapeutically sound interventions is key.

Therapeutic Factors

For decades, practitioners and group members alike have attempted to identify how groups that benefit their respective clientele work. Irv Yalom has identified 11 therapeutic factors that influence the process of change and recovery in group participants. These factors are as follows: (1) instillation of hope; (2) universality; (3) imparting information; (4) altruism; (5) development of socializing techniques; (6) imitative behavior; (7) catharsis; (8) the corrective recapitulation of the primary family group; (9) existential factors; (10) group cohesiveness; and (11) interpersonal learning (Yalom, 2005). Each one of these factors deserves extensive discussion. However, for the purposes of this chapter, a brief review of the meaning of each of these factors will be provided.

Instillation of Hope

The *instillation of hope* refers to faith gained in the group process. Regardless of one's diagnosis, condition, or issues, many feel a sense of hopelessness about their situation. While common wisdom dictates that if an individual will buy in to the group process positive outcomes will likely occur, this rarely happens for most individuals. The group member needs to see some form of proof that this process will be beneficial. Regardless of professional qualifications or the reputation of the establishment, people usually need to feel some personal connection or rationale for investing in the group process. Seeing someone else benefit from a process in the group like a technique or relating to another group member can significantly impact an individual's investment in the group and greatly improve the chances that positive outcomes will occur. If the individual can see someone else benefit or experience some feeling of benefit from the group, an instillation of hope will occur. This increases the potential for benefit immeasurably.

Universality

Many group participants have gone through life with an overwhelming sense of hopelessness and isolation. Each potential group member has indeed experienced his or her own unique and often tragic life story. This individual is convinced that his or her own uniqueness has placed him or her out of the reach of help. When group members participate in groups, a sense of relief can occur when the individual discovers that she or he is not alone in the experience or set of circumstances. This concept is referred to as *universality*. Upon realizing that the individual is not alone, he or she is immediately put in a position of buying into a process of self-discovery and, hopefully, growth.

Imparting Information

Imparting information occurs when a facilitator provides didactic instruction or very specific information in group. This is much like a teacher lecturing to a classroom of students. Information can also be delivered when a fellow group member or the facilitator provides advice or feedback. While this is a therapeutic factor, information giving can also be detrimental to a group. Advice or information provided without the development of relationship often falls on deaf ears. Meaningful interactions that do not involve guiding a group member are recommended before providing direction. The group member has to feel a sense of investment or a sense of caring about the outcome of the group experience. Once this occurs, imparting information through feedback or even advice-giving becomes possible.

Altruism

Altruism is a factor in group process that relies on the group members helping one another. As many great leaders and thinkers have eluded, those who help others appear to find purpose, meaning, and even happiness in life. Opportunities for altruistic endeavors present themselves over the course of the group experience. Often these opportunities come in the form of supportive, honest feedback. The sense of helping another can result in boosting self-esteem. Additionally, helping others pulls the individual out of self-defeating self-absorption. This is critical in the process of changing maladaptive thinking and behavior.

Development of Socializing Techniques

The *development of socializing techniques* involves the group member in learning how to develop new and more adaptive skills when interacting with others. This can be facilitated through practicing a certain skill in the group, but perhaps the most impactful form of this factor is feedback provided by other group members. Feedback from peers is often more valued than the feedback of any expert or facilitator.

Imitative Behavior

A group also offers an opportunity for vicarious learning. The group member may begin to imitate the behavior of another group member. It is important to note that the group facilitator and group members may never know what behavior is imitated. A group member may respect a certain skill or quality of another in the group and practice that skill or quality for her- or himself. This therapeutic factor is referred to as *imitative behavior.*

Catharsis

Catharsis is a factor that occurs in a group that refers to the expression of emotions. For whatever reason, the group member may not have experienced this opportunity to simply vent. This is an impactful factor for growth in the individual. While expression of affect is especially useful for the self-injurer, it is worth noting that venting is not the end of lasting change, but the beginning. It is easy to assume that because one expresses his or her feelings and thoughts, even in a dramatic way, that individual can now stop dysfunctional behavior and thinking. This is rarely the case. Once this has occurred, the individual has released energy around those thoughts and feelings and now change is more likely. In any case, external expression of internal conflict and affect followed by acceptance and understanding by fellow group members can lead to unparalleled growth.

The Corrective Recapitulation of the Primary Family Group

In group psychotherapy, group members most likely interact with one another as was learned in his or her first group experience, the family. Group members are not necessarily conscious of this reality. Of course there can be facilitative social qualities that were learned in the primary group. There can also exist more negative or maladaptive qualities and behaviors. The group can function as a vehicle to exercise these behaviors and qualities. The group facilitator can assist the group member in identifying those qualities and behaviors that are useful in proceeding through life and those that are not. The other group members are useful in bringing these qualities to the surface. Usually the individual learns of his or her behaviors unique to primary family interaction through interacting with other group members. These group members can also be facilitative in working through these sometimes maladaptive qualities and behaviors.

Existential Factors

As the group process continues and expands, a certain subtle quality may arise. Hopefully as members become more trusting with one another through shared experiences and activities in the group, the capacity to simply be with fellow group members may develop. Through these shared experiences and learning how to relate to others, the individual can begin to understand that life can be unfair and unjust. Ultimately, no matter how much support the individual receives, many of life's challenges must be faced alone. Once the individual can face this reality, then the process of living more authentically can take place. Living authentically might be translated to mean the individual can decipher the important things in life for her or him and not become overburdened by other realities. This usually happens after trust and experience in the group have developed.

Group Cohesiveness

Group cohesiveness refers to the group member feeling a sense of connection to and warmth for the other group members. This promotes the group member genuinely caring about the welfare of the group and its members. The individual and fellow group members are invested in others experiencing change and support to equal degree of their own. Yalom promotes the vital importance of this therapeutic factor. It is integral to the development and ultimate success of the group.

Interpersonal Learning

The therapeutic factor of interpersonal learning goes hand in hand with group cohesiveness. Group members learn to value the interpersonal relationships experienced in the group. These relationships are important.

They are the practice field through which true interpersonal learning occurs. Without these relationships, the degree of understanding how one operates in relationships outside the group would be significantly diminished.

Yalom's therapeutic factors have been in place for decades and have served as a building block for understanding the mechanisms and benefits of the group experience. For the self-injuring individual, many (if not all) of these factors are essential for growth. The social component relating to others, learning how to cope with stressors and overwhelming feelings, universality, and catharsis are just a few therapeutic factors that the self-injurer might benefit.

WHAT IS POTENTIALLY HEALING ABOUT THIS APPROACH?

Research suggests that group interventions seem to correlate with reduced NSSI symptoms. In other words, this medium seems to work in helping the self-injurer. However, there does not appear to be definitive evidence that groups are more or less therapeutic than individual therapy. Each modality appears to possess therapeutic qualities that benefit the self-injurious patient. Clearly, therapy works. Studies are inconclusive on exactly which modality might work best. One reason group is indicated when working with a variety of psychological distress (e.g., depression, anxiety, chemical dependency) is that the group reaches out to more individuals at one time. This speaks to the practicality of the group experience. However, what is considered therapeutic or helpful about a group for the self-injurious member? A variety of concepts run across successful therapeutic groups regardless of the designated topic of the group. Perhaps some of the benefits of a group can be found in these constructs.

Confidentiality

The concept of confidentiality is discussed at length at the beginning of most therapeutic groups. Confidentiality basically means that whatever is discussed or done in the group will stay within the group. This concept is also a part of individual counseling. However, in individual work, only the client and the therapist must maintain confidentiality. If someone talked, it wouldn't be difficult to discover who did. In groups, confidentiality cannot be promised. There are too many people to control. It cannot be done. The trust that confidentiality will be maintained is shared by the group members. This requires a level of responsibility on each of the group members. This responsibility has a therapeutic quality to it. In many cases, the self-injurious group member may not come from an environment in which such a responsibility is asked. In many cases, this individual may not be trusted at all but be seen as a problem or someone that is incapable of managing components of daily living. In this case, trust that confidentiality can be maintained and that the power to maintain it is given to the group members is therapeutic. The group member is an entrusted member of an important vessel, the group.

Another angle is in play. If each group member believes that discussions and activities will remain in the room even if something provocative or unpopular might be shared, the group can be deemed a safe place to be vulnerable and open. This may be a rare and cherished opportunity for the group member with issues like self-harming behaviors, depression, anxiety, substance abuse, or dysfunctional eating. For many individuals dealing with these types of issues, fulfilling the role of a troubled person who cannot be trusted and should be monitored at all times is all too familiar. In a confidential environment like a group, dignity and individual power can be bolstered in the individual.

An Environment of Change

In his powerful demonstration of an inpatient therapy group, Irv Yalom (1990) asks one of his patients in a group meeting what she would like to work on. When the patient, Rose, answers, "Depression, I guess," Yalom points out that depression is certainly important but too big to handle in one group meeting. He then helps her define an agenda of battling her depression by interacting with the other group members within the group. Rose experiences many opportunities to address her fellow group members, and by the end of a single group, she appears to experience a shift in mood and how she interacts with others.

A group certainly allows the individual the space to discuss his or her designated problem (i.e., self-injury). However, the group provides the opportunity to discuss the problem but also provides an opportunity to address a solution. Individual counseling offers only the therapist with whom to practice skills. In a group, the group member experiences the opportunity to test reality through experimentation or practice of coping skills, confrontation, or whatever may need to be explored. This combined with supportive feedback by fellow group members and the facilitator can lead to impactful realizations of empowerment and paradigm shift for the individual.

Universality

Previously, the therapeutic factor of universality was discussed. The self-injuring individual whether adolescent or adult is likely to be struggling with feelings of uniqueness and depression. In normal development, adolescents struggle with the concept of personal fable. This means the individual believes she or he is the center of attention for all around him or her. Additionally, personal fable promotes the belief that no one could possibly understand one's unique and personal feelings (Elkind, 1967). This already challenging reality can be exacerbated by feelings of depression and anxiety often experienced by the self-injurer. Furthermore, self-injurious behavior and comorbid behaviors like bingeing and purging or abuse of substances can only add to the feelings of self-loathing and uniqueness.

The group can provide a strong combatant to the condition of uniqueness. In fact, it provides an avenue for the group member to discover that she or he is not alone in his or her uniqueness. By observing others, hearing others' stories, interacting with fellow group members, and receiving supportive and even understanding feedback can promote feelings of universality. The individual can learn that he or she is not as distorted and shamefully unique as previously imagined. This is a component of group work that cannot be equaled in individual counseling. While the individual therapist and the self-injurious patient can develop a strong and facilitative relationship, there is nothing like the influence of one's peers, especially if those peers can provide understanding and support.

WHAT IS POTENTIALLY HARMFUL ABOUT THIS APPROACH?

Therapeutically speaking, the group experience is like none other. It can provide a multitude of therapeutic possibilities. However, it is important to note that group is not for everyone. Potential group members with overwhelming feelings of shame or extreme moods may feel unsafe in a group setting. It is possible that an individual may assign judgments that other group members are making well before those members have an opportunity to prove otherwise. This can immediately shut off the group member and promote hiding out in the group and not participating altogether. With little conclusive research on positive outcomes in groups for self-injurers, some are dubious about the benefits of a group with this issue. In fact, some members of the mental health community strictly promote the use of individual therapy in working with the self-injuring patient.

Additionally, other diagnoses that may coexist with self-injury may make groups a difficult prospect for all involved. Untreated disorders like major depression, anxiety disorders, schizophrenia, and multiple personality disorder are just some diagnoses that may coexist with self-injury that can decrease the probability of positive outcome in a group for the individual and fellow group members alike. Of course, the individual is not just her or his diagnosis. Each case would have to be considered individually. A therapist facilitating a group cannot make a fully informed decision about an individual benefitting from a group by simply reading diagnoses from an intake form. If possible, screening interviews are quite helpful in determining if the individual will benefit from the group experience. Diagnoses should not be about creating a bias toward the individual, but helping determine the best means of treatment.

A group can also be a breeding ground for triggering behaviors. It is imperative that group not be used to indulge in swapping stories. The process of one-upping other group members can serve to glorify the behavior and actually promote its use. It is important to make groups facilitative and movement-oriented. Stretches of group time in which group members tell stories can appear to promote interaction and universality to the untrained eye. However, caution must be infused. When storytelling occurs, the therapist is tasked with bringing the group back to therapeutically solid intervention. For example, if a group member begins to tell a nostalgic story about his or her self-injurious behavior, the therapist must know when to focus on the meaning of the story shared, how the behavior affects the individual, and how to involve other group members in relating to inner experience of the individual in question. This takes a tremendous amount of skill and insight on the part of the therapist.

Online Group Formats

There is no denying that the Internet and, consequently, digital methods of connecting have significantly affected how people communicate with one another. As society becomes more connected through the digital world, the reality that people will develop intimate and meaningful relationships online without meeting face to face with another person is an inescapable reality. One hope is that technology will continue to improve in quality of relational connection. At the time of this publication, it is hard to imagine that online interaction can truly replace the tangible reality of face-to-face, real-time contact. However, it is happening as we exist in this moment.

The development of blogs, message forums, online chat rooms, and social networks like Facebook has continued to improve in quality and multiply in breadth. This is the case for many mental health conditions. A query into a search engine of choice is all that is needed to find chat rooms on subjects like depression, anxiety, posttraumatic stress disorder (PTSD), bipolar disorder, alcoholism, drug addiction, personality disorders, autism, or Asperger's syndrome, and many more can be easily accessed. Of course, an equal number of chat rooms, blogs, and informational sites exist for family and friends of any of the previously mentioned disorders and conditions.

There is an equal number of these online resources for self-injury. Statistically, youth and young adults are the most prevalent groups to use self-injury as a coping mechanism. Interestingly enough, this is also the group that makes the greatest use of access to the Internet and digital resources (Lewis, Heath, Michael, & Duggan, 2012). This has prompted an increase in research of online resources for self-injury (Lewis, Heath, St. Denis, & Noble, 2011). In fact, the Internet is the preferred method of connection and communication for many youth and especially those youth who employ self-injury.

Benefits of Online Resources

Current research suggests that many self-injurious individuals who participate in online resources use those resources as an adjunct to professional help. In fact, some report a decline in self-injurious behavior upon making use of these resources. These individuals also report an appreciation for online controls like intolerance for triggering language by participants in the online group format. Participants also report a consistent understanding of self-injury with the primary conceptualization being that the individual has a relationship with self-injury and that the behavior serves to provide comfort and manage emotions. These individuals also reported an appreciation for the supportive nature of the online format. This suggests that the primary purpose of these resources was fulfilled.

Overall, family and members of the mental health community can rest assured that many of these online resources maintain the best intentions for those who participate. Also, this research suggests there is hope that many who participate in these online resources intend to manage or stop self-injurious behavior altogether. With an attitude of getting help and support and use of these resources, there is an indication that they can be used responsibly (Haberstroh & Moyer, 2012; Lewis et al., 2012).

Potential Deficits of Online Resources

Hope certainly exists for the use of online resources with those who desire to stop the behavior. There are some tangible reasons for concern, however. To begin, current research suggests these resources lack immediacy. Many participants report a discrepancy in time between the original posts and actual responses or feedback to the posts. This prompts concerns for the self-injurious individual looking for immediate feedback. This is one benefit of face-to-face group process. Immediate feedback is available to the individual. Unfortunately, lag time in feedback can actually promote self-injury or other maladaptive coping behaviors (Haberstroh & Moyer, 2012; Lewis et al., 2011).

Online resources appear promising in terms of providing support and understanding for those who would not normally seek them in public forums (e.g., support groups, counseling or psychotherapy groups). However, a sense of connectedness is lacking. Connectedness can mean interacting with others while managing one's internal process and even communicating one's experience in the moment.

For example, Mandy participates in an outpatient counseling group for women. During one particular group encounter, she shares that she thinks bulimia or any eating "issue" is "stupid." "How can someone eat until they throw-up? I mean, come on! Just get a grip!" she exclaims. Several other women appear affected by Mandy's remarks. One group participant confronts Mandy. "Mandy, I have actually struggled with bulimia for a great deal of my life. I am really angry that you have said that." Mandy immediately feels overwhelming anxiety. She could not imagine that her comments would be so impactful. "How could I have said that!?!", she remarks to herself. The counselor, recognizing an opportunity for growth, reflects, "Mandy, it is pretty obvious that Rachel's comments to you really surprised you. I imagine you feel really embarrassed right now." Mandy can barely muster a response. When she feels this kind of anxiety, she frequently cuts to relieve the stress. She can't do that and is forced to respond out of her own sense of embarrassment. "Yeah," she says, "I just want to crawl under the chair. I didn't think about what I was saying." The counselor asks if there is anything she wants to say to the group. Mandy goes on to talk about her embarrassment, fear, and loneliness in the moment. She even goes on to discuss her sister's struggles with eating disorder. She apologizes to the group and then tells them that she will leave if that is what the group wants. Many of the group members respond visibly, shaking their heads, "No." The counselor asks Mandy if she would be willing to hear some feedback from the group. "I don't think they want you to go," the counselor states. Mandy then receives supportive and encouraging feedback for her willingness to share her feelings. Later group meetings provide Mandy the opportunity to discuss how she copes with feelings and begins to contemplate other methods of managing her emotions.

This kind of immediate feedback would be difficult online. Even if the individual receives an immediate response, it would be difficult to match the immediacy and quality of the interaction that Mandy experienced in her group experience. Individuals who are yearning for connection and understanding might very well receive it online, but it is limited. When experiencing an emotionally delicate state, the individual often needs connection through, not only, verbal interaction, connection through proximity. This kind of interaction can serve as ground to test reality and receive support.

CONCLUSION

This chapter has covered the use of group work with self-injurious behavior. While the research is inconclusive in how the self-injuring client benefits from group experiences, groups will continue to be an integral part of therapy especially in inpatient settings. Perhaps group and individual modalities can both provide unique and distinct benefits when working with self-injury. There are not many facilities devoted strictly to the treatment of self-injury. However, self-injury will frequently arise. Consumers are encouraged to screen for quality when seeking out treatment options. Hopefully, this chapter has provided insight into components, benefits, and limitations of group psychotherapy.

CHAPTER 9

Psychopharmacological Treatment of Self-Injury

Nonsuicidal self-injury has served as a perplexing issue for almost any individual involved in the process of care. Parents, close friends, primary care physicians, mental health professionals, and often the self-injurer him- or herself seek answers to the source of the behavior and, perhaps more importantly, how to treat it. Research suggests that the psychiatric community finds the behavior just as difficult to conceptualize and treat. One reason for this may be that there exists little empirical research to suggest one form of psychopharmacological treatment over another. To date, most research consists of case studies or small samples to provide a basis for procedure in treatment. This typically does not sit well with those tasked with providing the treatment. Most sound medical treatments are based on significant quantitative research. For example, treatments for diagnoses such as cancer or diabetes usually evolve as a result of years of numerous quantitative studies that identify promising treatment protocols. At this point, nonsuicidal self-injury has not been studied extensively enough to suggest one or any treatment procedures without some doubt of effectiveness.

For the purpose of this chapter, quantitative research may be defined as the collection of numerical data aimed at establishing any causal relationship between two or more variables. In this case, the effects of medication on the cessation of self-harming behaviors are studied. To say the least, researchers prefer large amount of data that provide validity and reliability to a certain form of treatment. Due to a dearth of research on the topic of psychopharmacological treatment of nonsuicidal self-injury, the medical community, particularly psychiatrists, possesses little assurance of a particular treatment protocol. And yet, these professionals often find themselves on the frontline of treatment.

There exist some single-case studies and anecdotal data that report favorable outcomes for psychopharmacological treatment of self-injury. However, these reports are varied in their respective opinions and, at times, contradict one another. This has created confusion and controversy around how to treat self-injury from a psychiatric perspective. This chapter will describe the process of assigning a psychopharmacological treatment to a case of nonsuicidal self-injury, as well as describe how this form of treatment may work in conjunction with other psychological protocols.

THE PURPOSE OF MEDICATION IN TREATING SELF-INJURY

To begin, defining the psychiatrist's task is in order. A psychiatrist is a medical doctor (MD) who specializes in the diagnosis and treatment of mental illness. More specifically, a psychiatrist is responsible for prescribing medications that are intended to treat symptoms of a mental disorder while also ensuring that physiological health is not compromised. For example, some antipsychotic medications have been found to raise blood sugar levels. This is an important consideration for those individuals who are managing type I or type II diabetes. In the case of diabetes, consistently high glucose levels can have devastating, if not fatal, effects. This is a complicated responsibility for psychiatrists. In many cases, the psychiatrist is in regular communication with the patient to ensure that this process goes accordingly. Many psychiatrists also perform at least some counseling, equipping their patients with coping skills to assist in management of emotional and cognitive challenges.

As nonsuicidal self-injury has only recently gained its own diagnosis in the DSM-5, it is still considered secondary to other diagnoses. For years, self-injury was considered a part of diagnostic criteria for borderline personality disorder. Many in the mental health profession still consider this when conceptualizing self-injury. The psychiatric community is no exception. In fact, literature suggests that personality disordered traits often accompany self-injurious behavior whether it is nonsuicidal or suicidal in nature. Self-injury gaining its own diagnosis certainly opens possibilities and expands thinking around the behavior for those tasked with treating it. It is no longer only a part of diagnostic criteria but its own diagnosis. No doubt this will result in greater study in treatment options. However, at this point, self-injury would not be considered a primary diagnosis from a psychiatric perspective. At the time of this publication, there is no Food and Drug Administration (FDA)-approved medication for treating self-injury. And yet psychiatrists are commonly faced with assisting the patient in managing the behavior. So, how can a psychiatrist conceptualize the behavior and, consequently, treat it?

The psychiatric community views self-injury similarly to the rest of the mental health community. Poor emotional self-regulation is often seen as the culprit when self-injury is presented. When assessing the patient, a psychiatrist is likely to complete an evaluation of the patient that includes the amount of time and frequency of self-injury, the depth or superficiality of the self-mutilation, the patient's medical history, and medication and/or treatment that has proven beneficial in the past (if any).

Another task for the psychiatrist is to identify which neurotransmitter system is likely affected when self-injury is present. Identifying the neurotransmitter system is important from a neurobiological perspective. If the system can be identified accurately, a proper medication can be prescribed. One of three neurotransmitter systems is usually involved: serotonin, opiate, or dopamine.

Serotonin

As previously discussed, the neurotransmitter serotonin is responsible for regulation of mood. Theoretically, when serotonin levels drop in the brain, the individual will experience depression and/or anxiety. Impulsive behavior is frequently associated with mood disorders. An impulsive behavior related to depression and anxiety is self-injury. Impulsive behavior is characterized by moving to action based on a sudden emotion or impulse. This suggests that when someone acts impulsively, the individual has not thought through the action.

For example, the self-injurer will commit a self-harming act shortly after experiencing emotional dysregulation. In other words, the individual experiences a stressor in the environment that stimulates feelings that are intolerable. Shortly thereafter, typically within 30 to 90 minutes, the individual will self-injure. This is classified as an impulsive act. Some self-injurers have described the time between a trigger like arguing with a teacher at school and the actual act of self-mutilation as a feeling of anxiety or uneasiness. There is an impulse to remove this feeling. Consequently, for the individual who has found self-harming behavior to serve as a means of coping, a cut, burn, or other form of self-mutilation will occur.

Studies have indicated that antidepressants like tricyclic, atypical, and selective serotonin reuptake inhibitors (SSRIs) can significantly affect impulsivity in self-injuring patients. In fact, antidepressants are often a frontline medication for those reporting self-injurious behavior coexisting with dysregulated mood like depression and anxiety. Antidepressants are found in four categories: monoamine oxidase inhibitors (MAOIs), tricyclic, SSRIs, and atypical.

MAOIs are the oldest form of antidepressants. First discovered in the 1950s, these medications were found to possess an antidepressant quality while being prescribed to tubercular patients. MAOIs have been found to have severe interactions with some forms of food and drinks that contain tyramine. Tyramine is a derivative of the amino acid tyrosine. Tyramine is typically ingested through food and drink like aged cheese, chocolate, beer, and wine. The primary concern in combining MAOIs and a tyramine-rich diet is the side effect of dangerously high blood pressure. Consequently, if an MAOI is prescribed by a physician, dietary intake must be closely monitored. These medications are also no longer endorsed by any pharmaceutical companies. Consequently, these drugs are rarely prescribed. Examples of MAOIs are phenelzine (Nardil), isocarboxazid (Marplan), and tranylcypromine (Parnate).

Tricyclic antidepressants are also an older form of the medication. Tricyclic antidepressants work by blocking absorption of serotonin and norepinephrine. By blocking the uptake of these neurotransmitters, they are more available for the brain to complete its numerous and varied processes. Tricyclics affect a myriad of physiological functioning. Consequently, they also promote a variety of side effects including dizziness and nausea, weight gain, and sexual dysfunction. Tricyclic antidepressants require approximately two weeks to fully enter one's system and begin effecting mood change. This form of antidepressant also can have significant side effects if abruptly discontinued. There are a variety of tricyclic medications including, but not limited to, amitriptyline (Elavil), Clomipramine (Anafranil), Desipramine (Norpramin), and doxepin (Sinequan).

SSRIs are a newer form of antidepressant. The way in which this antidepressant works is to prevent serotonin from naturally being reabsorbed. Theoretically, this leaves a high concentration of the neurotransmitter left in the synapse (or gap) between two cells. Consequently, there is more serotonin for the cells to use. SSRIs are often the frontline medication when self-injury presents itself as a symptom. In using SSRIs, fewer side effects have been reported than the previously mentioned forms of antidepressants. However, there still exist a garden variety of side effects including nausea and dizziness, weight gain, decrease in sexual desire, headaches, and increased anxiety. There are also reports of increased anxiety and suicidal ideation with the use of SSRIs. Like their predecessors, SSRIs come in a variety of forms including fluoxetine (Prozac), sertraline (Zoloft), paroxetine (Paxil), escitalopram (Lexapro), and citalopram (Celexa).

Atypical antidepressants are the newest form of the medication. These compounds affect the reuptake of serotonin and, in some forms of the medication, norepinephrine. Consequently, they are referred to as serotonin and norepinephrine reuptake inhibitors (SNRIs). The names of this form of antidepressant include duloxetine (Cymbalta), venlafaxine (Effexor), mirtazapine (Remeron), and trazodone (Desyrel). Bupropion (Wellbutrin) is another antidepressant that actually affects the reabsorption of norepinephrine and dopamine. Wellbutrin has been reported to be more stimulating than other forms of antidepressants and also appears to have less adverse effects on sexual functioning.

Studies have indicated that antidepressants can produce a marked effect on the propensity to self-injure. Antidepressants appear to target impulsivity and aggression in the self-injuring individual. These same studies indicate that there appears to be a strong link between impulsivity and aggression and self-injury. More study is needed to better understand how these mechanisms seem to relate to one another. But, nevertheless, antidepressants appear to be a valid component in treating self-injury.

Dopamine

While the dopamine system must be acknowledged, there exists little research. However, some research indicates a connection between self-injury and those dealing with Lesch-Nyhan syndrome. This disorder involves dysregulation of the dopamine system. Dopamine is associated with pleasure and reward within the individual.

Lesch-Nyhan syndrome is a disorder in which the individual (almost exclusively male) suffers from a deficiency of the enzyme hypoxanthine phosporibosyl transferase (HPRT). This leads to excessive uric acid production. Urate crystals are deposited throughout the peripheral organs and produce neurological, renal, and musculoskeletal complications. Developmental delay and mental retardation are some of these complications. The child appears to be developing normally for the first few months, but after about one year, the child develops involuntary movements. Self-injurious behavior in the form of self-biting of the lips, tongue, fingers, and shoulders is present. Typically, this behavior is treated with a combination of physical restraint, behavioral therapy, and, of course, pharmaceuticals. Pharmaceutical treatment specifically aimed at the self-injury can involve the use of benzodiazepines, neuroleptics,

antidepressants, and anticonvulsive medication. Examples of benzodiazepines are chlordiazepoxide (Librium) and diazepam (Valium). These medications have a sedative, antianxiety effect. Often they are prescribed for
anxiety, seizures, insomnia, and muscle spasms. This form of medication
has a disinhibiting effect on its users. Consequently, benzodiazepines are
typically not prescribed for impulsive self-injury as previously described.

Opiate

Many who employ self-injury report an analgesic quality to their
respective experience. In other words, when someone cuts her- or himself
accidentally, perhaps while cutting vegetables, he or she experiences
unwanted pain. When the self-injurer makes a cut, a hypoactive amount
of pain is experienced. The self-injurer often does not experience pain in
the same way. Pain sensitivity is decreased. One theory on pain desensiti-
zation in the self-injurer involves the experience of habitual childhood
abuse. It is thought that habitual sexual or physical abuse promotes high
levels of endogenous opioids. When this individual experiences stress into
adulthood, his or her pain threshold increases. He or she is able to experience more pain, and, consequently, acts of self-injury do not possess the
same level of pain as perceived by the non-self-injurer. Yet another theory
would point to an addiction to endogenous opioids. If the self-injurer
seeks relief from a stressor and a form of self-mutilation provides it, the
possibility exists that both theories could be plausible.

In this case, the opiate antagonist may be prescribed. An opiate antagonist may be defined as drugs that block the effects of adrenaline and other
endorphins. Coincidentally, these medications also block the effects of
opiates like heroin, methadone, and morphine. The drugs just listed block
pain and promote feelings of euphoria, making them incredibly popular
and addictive in their own right. The opiate antagonist blocks this effect
in the self-injurer who finds an analgesic quality to self-harming behavior.
Therefore, drugs like naltrexone and naloxone have been shown to have a
positive effect in treating the impulsive self-injurer.

Psychiatrists may also prescribe antipsychotics like risperidone
(Risperdal) and mood stabilizers like carbamazepine (Tegretol), valproic
acid (Depakote), and lithium (Lithobid) for self-injurious behavior. These
medications are regularly prescribed for regulating the mania and depressive
states that can be associated with schizophrenia and bipolar disorder.
Some studies have found these medications to be helpful in managing impulsive and aggressive self-injury. Of course, like any medication, side effects

are present and should be closely monitored by the individual and prescribing physician.

Smith (2005) recommends the following in regard to psychopharmacological treatment of self-injurious behavior. SSRIs are typically recommended as a first-response medication. Specifically, the medication is intended to address the impulsivity related to self-injury. Additionally, SSRIs are considered to have more benign side effects for most patients. Atypical antipsychotics are considered a second-line prescription. Lastly, anticonvulsant mood stabilizers are recommended. In conclusion, Omega-3 fatty acids, clonidine, and naltrexone have been considered as an adjunct medication in treating the impulsive nature of self-injury if resistant to other prescriptions.

As previously mentioned, SSRIs and atypical antidepressants may be the frontline prescription for addressing the impulsive qualities in self-injury. Unfortunately, by the time many self-injuring patients have entered the psychiatrist's office, they are already prescribed an antidepressant with little or no benefit. This is when one of the other choices that have been described might be indicated. Future research will no doubt better guide the prescribing physician on best choices. In the meantime, a strong relationship that promotes communication between the patient and psychiatrist must be cultivated so that benefits and deficits of medication may be identified. All medications possess some side effects. A trusting relationship between the patient and physician can help the individual determine how to best manage these effects and establish if changes in dosage or prescription should be made.

COMBINING MEDICATION AND THERAPY

The literature discussing self-injury appears dichotomous at this point in time. There exists an ever increasing body of research around pharmacologically treating the behavior. There is also more research that addresses treating self-injury from a psychotherapeutic perspective. However, there is little research that addresses a collaborative approach to self-injury. There are a variety of reasons for this. For one, each of these distinctly different areas of treatment is still developing their own respective protocols. The study of self-injury itself is still quite new and fraught with complicating variables in each discipline. There exists little agreement on exactly the proper course in psychotropic medication treatment. The same could certainly be said for psychotherapeutic treatment.

In the process of determining best practices in each discipline, the research has simply not been completed as of yet.

However, this does not mean that treatment is hopeless—far from it! Self-injury is being treated successfully on a regular basis. Typically, self-injury is still conceptualized as a comorbid condition usually with a mood disorder. This would make sense as this behavior is concerned with managing emotions. Many who are dealing with self-injury and desire treatment can get it. Furthermore, a relationship between the individual, her or his psychiatrist, and his or her therapist is quite common. Inpatient treatment settings have made use of the team approach to treatment for decades. Outpatient settings make teamwork more complicated in that a professional often cannot send a patient down the hallway. However, this approach is not only possible, but frequently facilitated. The difference between these settings concerns the level of responsibility placed on the patient. In an inpatient setting, the team takes a great deal of the responsibility in managing the patients' needs. Visiting with a psychiatrist, attending a scheduled individual session with a therapist, and even scheduling a meal time are all handled in-house, making it difficult for the patient to miss these crucial appointments. When the patient is solely responsible for making appointments and following through with treatment prescription, that patient must be motivated to make changes or they will not happen.

Psychiatrists and therapists can and often do refer to one another. Referrals are often made between these disciplines for a variety of issues, and self-injury is no exception. There are some psychiatrists who also conduct psychotherapy with their patients. However, to date, many psychiatrists are busy with prescription management for their patients and have little time to conduct therapy. In any case, those who practice self-injury are in need of new skills, support, and a place in which to practice newly developed skills regardless of medication prescription. Medication management is out of the skill set of the therapist unless that therapist is a psychiatrist. And most psychiatrists are not in a position to conduct long-term therapy with their patients. With this being said, a team approach to treatment would seem to be indicated.

A CASE EXAMPLE

Caleb is a 20-year-old male who has been self-injuring since his parents' divorce at age 13. In the seven years since the divorce, Caleb experienced tremendous change within the household. His father moved out of the house and saw Caleb about one weekend a month. Even though his father had more frequent visitation privileges, he did not exercise that right. When Caleb would inquire with his father about not visiting more often, his father would cite his overburdened work schedule. While Caleb's mother attended to his daily needs, she was experiencing her own grief around the divorce. Right after Caleb's parents had split, Caleb attempted to talk with his mother about his own feelings. Caleb's mother replied, "Of course you are hurt by your father leaving. I am hurt too. He isn't worth it, Caleb! Just put your dad out of your mind. He has never been there for either one of us." This shocked and confused Caleb. From that point on, he certainly loved and enjoyed his mother, but he never believed he could talk to her about his father. Soon after this, while looking through a drawer in his bedroom, Caleb found a pocket knife that his father had given him years back. He immediately opened the knife and tested its sharpness on a piece of typing paper. He was amazed at how the knife had retained its sharpness over the years in that drawer. He then placed the edge of the knife to his forearm with the intent of shaving off a section of hair. He accidentally cut into his forearm and quickly blood began to trickle down his arm. He was immediately drawn to the sight of the blood. He suddenly felt calm and warm. This began a regimen of making small cuts on the inside of his upper arm and calves. Over the course of the next year, Caleb's dad met someone, and they soon married. Caleb and his father saw less and less of each other until their interaction was reduced to seeing each other on holidays.

As years passed, Caleb went from an honor student in middle school to a slightly below-average student in high school. Caleb was attentive enough in school to pass his classes. He maintained friendships. However, Caleb appeared to lack motivation in school. He participated in no extracurricular activities. When the school day concluded, he would simply go home and participate in online gaming. Throughout high school, he would attend parties with friends where he would drink and occasionally smoke marijuana.

After graduating from high school, Caleb attended a local community college taking one or two classes per semester with no genuine motivation. He continued to use self-injury on a daily basis. He did not understand the reasons for his use of self-injury, but he knew that it felt better after he cut. One day while attending his annual physical, his physician noticed the deliberate cuts on the underside of his upper arm. After his physician inquired about the cuts, Caleb hesitantly admitted that he cut himself on occasion. A few days later, his physician's office called Caleb asking him to come in for another appointment. Caleb feared something unusual in his blood work so he immediately scheduled the appointment.

When he actually attended the appointment, he was surprised to learn that his physician did not call him in to discuss blood work results. His doctor expressed his concern about the fresh cuts and apparent scars from past cuts on Caleb's upper arms. At first, Caleb was angry that the doctor had worried him over such a minor concern. Caleb exclaimed, "Doctor, those are no big deal. They don't hurt me." His physician went on to ask questions about Caleb's mood. Caleb admitted to feelings of depression but did not believe he was suffering from anything more than laziness.

Caleb's physician provided a referral for a psychiatric visit. Caleb's physician asked if Caleb would follow through with the referral. Caleb did not like lying and he was even more uncomfortable with confrontation, so he agreed to the referral. Approximately two weeks later, Caleb attended an appointment with Dr. Watkins, a psychiatrist. In spite of his suspicion about psychology and fear that he would be sedated and put away in some sort of dungeon, Caleb found Dr. Watkins to be very personable. Caleb even felt himself liking Dr. Watkins. Dr. Watkins asked a series of questions about Caleb's life. He focused on Caleb's self-report of depression with his primary care physician. After discussing the depression symptoms, Dr. Watkins asked Caleb about the cuts in his arms. Caleb reported that this was a means of managing anxiety and feelings of uneasiness. Dr. Watkins asked Caleb to complete a few questionnaires to assist in a diagnosis for Caleb. After completing the questionnaires, Dr. Watkins suggested that Caleb met the criteria for depression. Caleb accepted the diagnosis. He even felt some relief that there was a name or diagnosis that matched his feelings. Dr. Watkins explained Caleb's options. He, of course, could go on without treating his depression, he could seek out a therapist for which Dr. Watkins could provide some referrals, or he could prescribe an antidepressant and see how Caleb responded to the medication. Caleb certainly didn't want to go to a therapist and he was tired of feeling so down all of the time, so he agreed to the prescription. After a number of days, Caleb noticed a change in his mood. He felt lighter. He then went to a follow-up visit approximately two weeks later and reported the results to Dr. Watkins. Dr. Watkins asked about the self-injury. Caleb said it really hadn't stopped completely although perhaps he was cutting a little less than before. Dr. Watkins suggested some coping strategies to help in regulating his emotions. After another visit with Dr. Watkins, Caleb was feeling well enough to do some of his own homework around self-injury. He had found numerous sites on the Internet with articles and blogs on self-injury. He reported that a lot of what he was reading really made sense to him, particularly information on cutting when feelings of anxiety or uneasiness arose. Caleb and Dr. Watkins discussed changing Caleb's prescription to another medication that had some favorable results in management of impulsiveness. Caleb agreed to the new prescription and then asked Dr. Watkins, "You told me on our first visit that you knew of a few therapists I could call. Do you still have their phone numbers?"

Conclusion

Caleb's case is not an unusual one. Many who practice self-injury are capable of leading productive lives, making a diagnosis sometimes difficult. In many cases, cuts are discovered by caring professionals like Caleb's primary care physician. This can lead to gently pushing the self-injurer to see a psychiatrist and/or a therapist. Which one of these mental professionals comes first is not usually the pressing issue. If all professionals are competent, the individual will likely be directed to appropriate professional help. The relationship between the patient and professional often tells the tale of success. When a solid relationship is in place, the individual trusts the psychiatrist (or other mental health professional) with well-guarded information. In any case, these relationships can take months and years to develop based on the patient's background and level of coping. Caleb is a relatively high-functioning young man. Nevertheless, he may maintain a relationship with his psychiatrist to manage his medication. He may also maintain an ongoing relationship with a therapist to process life events like grieving his parents' divorce and consequent shift in relationship with each parent, as well as continue to develop new emotional regulation skills.

PART III

Resources

Resources

Self-Injury Websites

The Cornell Research Program on Self-Injury and Recovery: www.selfinjury.bctr
.cornell.edu

Helpguide.org (Emotional and mental health): http://www.helpguide.org/articles/
anxiety/cutting-and-self-harm.htm

Information and Support for Self-Injurers: www.self-injury.net

S.A.F.E. Alternatives (Nationally recognized treatment approach, professional
network, and educational resource base): www.selfinjury.com

Self-Injury Outreach & Support: www.sioutreach.org

WebMD: http://www.webmd.com/mental-health/features/cutting-self-harm-signs-
treatment

Self-Injury Books

Adler, P., & Adler, P. (2011). *The Tender Cut: Inside the Hidden World of
Self-Injury.* New York: New York University Press.

Conterio, K., & Lader, W. (1998). *Bodily Harm: The Breakthrough Healing
Program for Self-Injurers.* New York, NY: Hyperion.

Favazza, A. R. (2011). *Bodies under Siege: Self-Mutilation, Nonsuicidal Self-
Injury and Body Modification in Culture and Psychiatry* (3rd ed.).
Baltimore, MD: The Johns Hopkins University Press.

Hollander, M. (2008). *Helping Teens Who Cut: Understanding and Ending Self-
Injury.* New York: The Guilford Press.

Khemlani-Patel, S., McVey-Noble, M., & Neziroglu, F. (2006). *When Your Child
Is Cutting: A Parent's Guide to Helping Children Overcome Self-Injury.*
Oakland, CA: New Harbinger.

Levenkron, S. (1998). *Cutting: Understanding and Overcoming Self-Mutilation.* New York, NY: W.W. Norton and Company.

Nock, M. (2009). *Understanding Nonsuicidal Self-Injury: Origins, Assessment, and Treatment.* Washington, DC: American Psychological Association.

Nock, M. (2014). *The Oxford Handbook of Suicide and Self-Injury.* Oxford: Oxford University Press.

Strong, M. (1999). *A Bright Red Scream.* New York: Penguin.

Walsh, B. W. (2012). *Treating Self-Injury: A Practical Guide* (2nd ed.). New York: Guilford Press.

Walsh, B., & Rosen, P. (1988). *Self-Mutilation: Theory, Research, and Practice.* New York: Guilford Press.

Research Articles

Andover, M. S., & Gibb, B. E. (2010). Non-suicidal self-injury, attempted suicide, and suicidal intent among psychiatric inpatients. *Psychiatry Research*, 178, 101–105.

Andover, M. S., Primack, J. M., Gibb, B. E., & Pepper, C. M. (2010). An examination of non-suicidal self-injury in men: Do men differ from women in basic NSSI characteristics? *Archives of Suicide Research*, 14, 79–88.

Barrocas, A. L., Hankin, B. L., Young, J. F., & Abela, J. R. Z. (2012). Rates of nonsuicidal self-injury in youth: Age, sex, and behavioral methods in a community sample. *Pediatrics*, doi: 10.1542/peds.2011-2094.

Bryan, C., & Bryan, A. (2014). Nonsuicidal self-injury among a sample of United States military personnel and veterans enrolled in college classes. *Journal of Clinical Psychology*, 70, 874–885.

Claes, L., Klonsky, E. D., Muehlenkamp, W., Kuppens, P., & Vandereycken, W. (2010). The affect-regulation function of nonsuicidal self-injury in eating-disordered patients: Which affect states are regulated? *Comprehensive Psychiatry*, 51, 386–392.

Claes, L., Soenens, B., Vansteenkiste, M., & Vandereycken, W. (2012). The scars of the inner critic: Perfectionism and nonsuicidal self-injury in eating disorders. *European Eating Disorders Review*, 20, 196–202.

Gonzalez, A. H., & Bergstrom, L. (2013). Adolescent nonsuicidal self-injury (NSSI) interventions. *Journal of Child and Adolescent Psychiatric Nursing*, 26, 124–130.

Haberstroh, S., & Moyer, M. (2012). Exploring an online self-injury support group: Perspectives from group members. *The Journal for Specialists in Group Work*, 37(2), 113–132.

Hamza, C. A., Stewart, S. L., & Willoughby, T. (2012). Examining the link between nonsuicidal self-injury and suicidal behavior: A review of the literature and an integrated model. *Clinical Psychology Review, 32*, 482–495.

Turner, B. J., Austin, S. B., & Chapman, A. L. (2014). Treating nonsuicidal self-injury: A systematic review of psychological and pharmacological interventions. *Canadian Journal of Psychiatry, 59*(11), 576–585.

DOCUMENT 1

The following is a section of a self-injury fact sheet authored by Amanda Purington and Janis Whitlock. It is a collaboration of work between Cornell University, University of Rochester, and the New York State Center for School Safety. The authors provide an excellent, concise, and therapeutically sound perspective on how to approach the self-injuring adolescent. This section serves as a useful cheat sheet for the concerned individual.

APPROACHING SELF-INJURY FROM A YOUTH DEVELOPMENT PERSPECTIVE

- Self-injury is most common in youth having trouble coping with anxiety. It is important to focus on skill building in individual youth, and to identify and remedy the environmental stressors that trigger self-injury.
- Self-injury is most often a silent, hidden practice aimed at either squelching negative feelings or overcoming emotional numbness. Being willing to listen to the self-injurer while reserving shock or judgment encourages them to use their voice rather than their body as a means of self-expression.
- Self-injury serves a function. An important part of treatment is helping youth to find other, more positive ways to accomplish the same

psychological and emotional outcome, i.e. explicitly teach coping skills.

- Assessment and treatment should seek to understand why youth self-injure and then build on the strengths youth already possess.

Source: Amanda Purington and Janis Whitlock. *Approaching Self-Injury from a Youth Development Perspective.* Self-Injury Fact Sheet, ACT for Youth Center of Excellence. Online at http://actforyouth.net/resources/rf/ rf_selfinjury_0804.pdf. Used by permission.

DOCUMENT 2

The following document is a general fact sheet concerning self-injury found through a website called www.rethink.org. Much of the information is very useful and can be found in a variety of periodicals. However, the following question and answer is uniquely beneficial for those who are fearful and confused concerning how to share about their self-injury. Pointers are provided. Perhaps the most helpful quality of this document is that it encourages the self-injurer to take responsibility for the behavior and be accepting of those who may be confused by the behavior.

10. How can I tell my family and friends if I have a problem with self-harming?

If you self-harm, you might feel that no-one else does this. You might think that you are the only one who can understand why you do it. This can make you feel more alone and could make your self-harm worse.

Sharing your experiences can play an important part in your recovery. Eventually you may decide to talk to somebody about what has happened. This doesn't necessarily have to be in person, it might be easier to write it in a letter.

Here are a few pointers that people have found helpful:

- Be sensitive to the other person's feelings: Remember that it could be hard for your friend or relative to hear that you are harming your-self. They may feel guilty about what they could or could not have done to help.
- Explain that you are telling them because you love them: Explain that you opening up to them is positive and that it is because you love and trust them, not because you are trying to punish or manipulate them.

- Pick a place that is private and allow plenty of time: Pick a place where you will not be interrupted. Your friend or relative may need time to take everything in or they may want to ask you questions and talk more.
- Don't tell others in anger: It is best to tell your friend or relative when you are calm. Try to take things gently and don't blame them for your self-harm.
- Consider having someone else present: If you have a friend or therapist who understands self-harm you might want them to be there too. They might be able to help you tell your friend or relative and answer questions.
- Provide as much information as you can: The more someone knows about something, the less they fear it. Many people have the wrong idea about self-harm. Let your friend or relative know where they can find out more or who they can contact for support. Try and be as well informed as you can so that you can answer their questions.
- Be willing and prepared to answer their questions: You might want to think about the questions your friend or relative will ask and try to put together your answer. You should have a good idea of what you want to do about your self-harm and perhaps what you want them to do. Decide what you feel comfortable to talk about and what you are not.
- You don't need to go into a lot of detail in the first conversation: Avoid describing your self-harm in detail when you first tell your friend or relative. You can give them better descriptions if they need it.

Source: Rethink.org. Self-Harm Fact Sheet. Online at www.rethink.org/resources/s/self-harm-factsheet.

DOCUMENT 3

The following article provides an impressive reference list. The reader may note that many of the references found in this article are also seen in this text. In addition to the reference list, the article provides a concise and informative description of self-harm. In conclusion, the article succinctly outlines some of the common myths around self-injury. Note that the article was written prior to the release of the DSM-5. Self-injury actually does possess its own proposed diagnostic criteria.

MYTHBUSTER: SORTING FACT FROM FICTION ON SELF-HARM

By Faye Scanlan and Rosemary Purcell

What is self-harm?

Self-harm occurs when people deliberately hurt their bodies. The most common type of self-harm among young people is cutting (1). Other types include burning the skin until it marks or bleeds, picking at wounds or scars, self-hitting and pulling hair out by the roots (2). At the more extreme end of the spectrum, self-harm can include breaking bones, hanging and deliberately overdosing on medication (3).

There are other deliberate behaviours that can be harmful to one's health that are not normally included in the definition of self-harm. These include self-starving, binge drinking, smoking or other drug use and dangerous driving.

How many young people self-harm?

Research suggests that 6–7% of young Australians (aged 15–24) have self-harmed in any 12-month period, while over 12% report having done so at some point in their life (4–5). Self-harm is more common after the onset of puberty [6]. The average age at which self-harm first occurs is 12–14 years (7) and, in adolescents, it is more common among girls than boys (8). However, self-harm can occur in anyone, regardless of their age, gender, socio-economic status or culture/ethnicity.

Self-harm often goes unnoticed. It is commonly done in private and most young people who self-harm don't seek help or come to the attention of health services (e.g. 1,4,9).

Why do people self-harm?

Most self-harm is in response to intense pain, distress, or overwhelming negative feelings, thoughts or memories (e.g. 2,10–13). Although young people who self-harm might say that they want to die, the driving force behind their behaviour is often more to do with expressing their distress and desire to escape from troubling situations (14). It is usually a build up of negative experiences/stresses rather than any one single event or experience that triggers self-harm in young people (15).

Young people who self-harm may feel that it helps to relieve their distress and bring some sense of relief in the short term (12). However this feeling of relief typically doesn't last because the problems causing the distress are not being addressed. For some young people self-harm is a 'once off' event, but for others (over 50% who self-harm) it can become repetitive (16–18). Most young people who repeatedly self-harm say they never thought they would come to rely on it as a way to cope with their feelings (13). Many realise that, in the long term, self-harm is not an effective coping mechanism, but find it hard to give up. Often, they are not able to find other ways to cope with their distress (e.g. talking with somebody they can trust).

Some young people who repeatedly self-harm may experience the behaviour as being 'addictive' (e.g. 13). It is important to respect this viewpoint, and understand that, for these young people, recovery is not as simple as 'just stopping'. Often a person can stop self-harming only when they have developed more effective ways of coping with their distress. This process usually takes time. Initially the focus may need to be on helping the young person to reduce their level of self-harm rather than asking them to give it up immediately. However, with time and appropriate support, many young people do recover and stop self-harming (13).

Some common triggers of self harm are (14):

- Difficulties or disputes with parents, other family members or peers
- School or work problems
- Difficulties with boyfriends or girlfriends
- Physical health problems
- Depression
- Bullying
- Low self esteem
- Sexual problems
- Alcohol and drug abuse

Self-harm is more common than people may think. About 12% of young people in Australia report having self-harmed at some point in their life.

What are the most common myths surrounding self-harm?

There are many myths surrounding self-harm, which makes it hard to separate fact from fiction. It can be very confusing and difficult to understand, both to the person who is self-harming and to their friends and family (13). Raising the topic of self-harm can bring up uncomfortable feelings including fear, guilt, and shame (13,19).

Some of the most common myths around self-harm are:

- "Self-harm is an attempt at suicide"
- "It's just attention seeking"
- "It's an 'emo'/'goth' thing"

- "If you self-harm it means you're mentally ill"
- "People who self-harm have borderline personality disorder"

These are myths, not fact. But even as myths, they can be very powerful and impact not only on young people who self-harm, but also on those around them.

MYTH: "Self-harm is an attempt at suicide"

Often what frightens people most about self-harm is the assumption that the person is trying to kill themselves. This is not true. In the vast majority of cases, self-harm is a coping mechanism, not a suicide attempt (2–3,12). It may seem counter-intuitive, but in many cases, people use self-harm as a way to stay alive rather than end their life (2,13,17).

It is important to understand that self-harm is mostly an attempt to *hurt*, not to kill oneself. However there is a relationship between self-harm and suicide that does need to be considered. Sometimes people injure themselves more seriously than they intend to, and this can put their life at risk. Young people who self-harm are also at a much higher risk of attempting suicide at some time in the future than those who don't self-harm, even if they're not suicidal at the time (7). This doesn't mean they *will* attempt suicide, but rather that their *risk* is higher. It is important to encourage anyone who is self-harming to seek help from a health professional to address any underlying emotional problems (e.g. depression or anxiety).

MYTH: "It's just attention seeking"

Self-harm is not about attention seeking. Most young people who self-harm go to great lengths to draw as little attention as possible to their behaviour by self-harming in private and by harming parts of the body that are not visible to others (12–13). Even those closest to the young person are often unaware of it. One study found that the rates of self-harm reported by young people were three times higher than their parents estimated (20). Concealing self-harm can be a big burden for young people and can affect their day-to-day life. For example, it can determine what clothes they can wear (to cover up cuts or scars), limit their activities (e.g. not going to the beach or swimming) or cause them to avoid physical or intimate relationships in which someone might become aware of their self-harm (13).

Rarely, threats of self-harm or actual self-harm might be used to achieve a certain aim. This is often called 'manipulative behaviour'. Most of the time people self-harm in an attempt to change how they are feeling, rather than trying to get attention from, or manipulate, other people (2,11–12,17,21).

MYTH: "It's a fashion, a trend or an 'emo' thing"

Self-harm is not a new behaviour that arrived with a certain subculture or 'trend' amongst young people. Mental health professionals have been studying and treating self-harm for decades (e.g. 22). Despite this, self-harm has been and continues to be associated with certain subcultures resulting in stereotyped beliefs that only 'certain kinds of people' self-harm. Recently the 'emo' trend has received attention as being associated with depression, self-harm and suicide (23). A national inquiry into self-harm among young people in the UK found no evidence to suggest it was associated with any particular youth subculture (13).

The term 'emo' was originally used to describe a style of music known as 'emotive rock', which used expressive and often confessional lyrics. Today the term is used more broadly to describe a fashion style and personality traits such as being emotional, sensitive, shy, introverted, or angst-ridden (24).

MYTH: "If someone self-harms, they must have a mental illness or a personality disorder"

Self-harm is a behaviour or symptom, not a disorder or an illness. Self-harming behaviour is strongly suggestive of an underlying psychological or emotional problem (7,25), but many young people who self-harm do not meet the criteria for any specific mental illness diagnosis.

Borderline Personality Disorder (BPD) is the only mental health disorder for which self-harm is a diagnostic feature. As a result, young people are sometimes labeled as having BPD simply because they self-harm (19). In fact, only a small minority of young people who self-harm meet the diagnostic criteria. Self-harming behaviour alone should never result in the assumption that a person has BPD (10). BPD should only be diagnosed following a comprehensive assessment (26).

Want to know more?

For more reliable information about self-harm including factsheets, young people's stories of their experiences of self-harming and recovery, and information on how and where to get help check out the following websites: headspace.org.au and reachout.com.au

The Royal Australian and New Zealand College of Psychiatrists Guidelines on Self-harm are also helpful to young people and their carers (http://www.ranzcp.org/resources/clinical-practice-guidelines.html)

For practical tips on how to approach somebody who may be self-harming read the Mental Health First Aid Guidelines for Non-Suicidal Self-Injury (www.mhfa.com.au)

REFERENCES

1. Madge N., Hewitt A., Hawton K., De Wilde E. J., Corcoran P., Fekete S., Van Heeringen K., De Leo D. & Ystgaard M. (2008) Deliberate self-harm within an international community sample of young people: comparative findings from the child and adolescent self-harm in Europe (CASE) study. *J Child Psychol Psychiatry*, 49(6): p. 667–77.
2. Klonsky D. E. (2007) The functions of deliberate self-injury: A review of the evidence. *Clin Psychol Review*, 27(2): p. 226–39.
3. Skegg K. (2005) Self-harm. *Lancet*, 366(9495): p. 1471–83.
4. De Leo D. & Heller T.S. (2004) Who are the kids who self-harm? An Australian self-report school Survey. *Med J Aust*, 181(3): p. 140–44.
5. Schweitzer R., Klayich M. & McClean J. (1995). Suicidal ideation and behaviours among university students in Australia. *Aust NZ J Psychiatry*, 29(3): p. 473–79.
6. Patton G.C., Hemphill S.A., Beyers J.M., Bond L., Toumbourou J.W., McMorris B.J. & Catalano R.F. (2007) Pubertal Stage and Deliberate Self-Harm in Adolescents. *J Am Acad Child Adolescent Psychiat*, 46(4): p. 508–14.
7. Jacobson C.M. & Gould M. (2007) The epidemiology and phenomenology of non-suicidal self-injurious behavior among adolescents: A critical review of the literature. *Arch Suicide Res*, 11(2): p. 129–47.
8. Hawton K., Rodham K., Evans E. et al. (2002) Deliberate self-harm in adolescents: self report survey in schools in England. *BMJ*, 325(7374): p. 1207–11.
9. Fortune S., Sinclair J. & Hawton K. (2008) Help-seeking before and after episodes of self-harm: a descriptive study in school pupils in England. *BMC Public Health*, 8: p. 369.
10. NICE (2004) *Self-harm: The short-term physical and psychological management and secondary prevention of self-harm in primary and secondary care* (No. CG16). London: National Institute for Health and Clinical Excellence.
11. Scoliers G., Portzky G., Madge N. et al. (2009) Reasons for adolescent deliberate self-harm: a cry of pain and/or a cry for help? Findings from the child and adolescent self-harm in Europe (CASE) study. *Soc Psychiatry Psychiatr Epidemiol*, 44(8): p. 601–07.
12. Nock M.K., Prinstein M.J & Sterba S.K. (2009) Revealing the form and function of self-injurious thoughts and behaviors: A real-time ecological assessment study among adolescents and young adults. *J Abnormal Psychol*, 118(4): p. 816–27.

13. Mental Health Foundation (2006) *Truth Hurts: Report of the National Inquiry into self-harm among young people*. London: Mental Health Foundation.
14. Hawton K. & James A. (2005) ABC of adolescence: Suicide and deliberate self-harm in young people. *BMJ*, 330: p. 891–94.
15. Fox C. & Hawton K. (2004) *Deliberate self-harm in adolescence*. London: Jessica Kingsley Publishers.
16. Ross S. & Heath N. (2002) A study of the frequency of self-mutilation in a community sample of adolescents. *J Youth Adolesc*, 31(1): p. 67–77.
17. Laye-Gindhu A. & Schonert-Reichl K.A. (2005). Non-suicidal self-harm among community adolescents: Understanding the "whats" and "whys" of self-harm. *J Youth Adolesc*, 34(5): p. 447–57.
18. Muehlenkamp J.J. & Gutierrez P.M. (2007) Risk for suicide attempts among adolescents who engage in non-suicidal self-injury. *Archives of Suicide Research*. 11(11): p. 12–23.
19. McAllister M. (2003) Multiple meanings of self-harm: A critical review. *Int J Ment Health Nurs*, 12(3): p. 177–85.
20. Meltzer H., Harrington R., Goodman R. & Jenkins R. (2001). *Children and adolescents who try to harm, hurt or kill themselves: A report of further analysis of the national survey of the mental health of children and adolescents in Great Britain in 1999*. London: Office for National Statistics.
21. Nock M.K. & Prinstein M.J. (2005). Contextual features and behavioral functions of self-mutilation among adolescents. *J Abnormal Psychol*, 114(1): p.140–46.
22. Graff H. & Mallin R. (1967) The syndrome of the wrist cutter. *Am J Psychiatry*, 124(1): p. 36–42.
23. *Music, youth subculture and self-harm* [Factsheet]. Christchurch: Canterbury Suicide Project, 23 July 2006.
24. *'Emo': From Wikipedia the free encyclopedia*. Accessed 20/01/2010 http://en.wikipedia.org/wiki/Emo.
25. Crowley P., Kilroe J. & Burke S. (2005) *Youth suicide prevention: an evidence briefing*. Dublin: Health Development Agency.
26. NICE (2009) *Borderline Personality Disorder: The NICE guideline on treatment and management*. London: National Institute for Health and Clinical Excellence.
27. *Mindframe – Reporting suicide and mental illness: a resource for media professionals*. Accessed 20/01/2010 http://www.mindframe-media.info/site/index.cfm?display=98031.
28. McDonald G., O'Brien L. & Jackson D. (2007) Guilt and shame: experiences of parents of self-harming adolescents. *J Child Health Care*, 11(4): p. 298–310.
29. Oldershaw A., Richards C., Simic M. & Schmidt U. (2008) Parents' perspectives on adolescent self-harm: qualitative study, *Br J Psychiatry*, 193(2): p. 140–44.

30. Centre of Excellence in Youth Mental Health (2009) Mythbuster-Suicidal Ideation: MYTH: *"Asking young people about suicidal thoughts or behaviours will only put ideas in their heads,"* Orygen Youth Health Research Centre.

ACKNOWLEDGEMENTS

headspace Mythbusters are prepared by the Centre of Excellence in Youth Mental Health. The series aims to unveil common myths that are contrary to the research evidence about mental health and substance use problems affecting young people. Experts on the topic have reviewed the summary before publication, including members of the headspace Youth National Reference Group (HYNRG). The authors would like to thank the members of HYNRG for their input on this Mythbuster.

Source: Faye Scanlan and Rosemary Purcell. *Mythbuster: Sorting Fact from Fiction on Self-Harm.* © Headspace National Youth Mental Health Foundation Ltd. This document is reproduced with the permission of headspace.

DOCUMENT 4

The following article conducts research concerning the Diagnostic and Statistical Manual for Mental Disorders, 5th Edition *and its recent inclusion of nonsuicidal self-injury as its own diagnosis. While the diagnosis is considered a "Condition for further study," it still proposes some significant changes in how nonsuicidal self-injury is conceptualized. The following article examines diagnostic and clinical correlates of this change in the DSM-5.*

PROPOSED DIAGNOSTIC CRITERIA FOR THE DSM-5 OF NONSUICIDAL SELF-INJURY IN FEMALE ADOLESCENTS: DIAGNOSTIC AND CLINICAL CORRELATES

By Tina In-Albon, Claudia Ruf, and Marc Schmid

Abstract

Nonsuicidal self-injury (NSSI) is included as conditions for further study in the DSM-5. Therefore, it is necessary to investigate the proposed diagnostic criteria and the diagnostic and clinical correlates for the validity of a diagnostic entity. The authors investigated the characteristics of NSSI disorder and the proposed diagnostic criteria. A sample of 73 female inpatient adolescents and 37 nonclinical adolescents (aged 13 to 19 years) was recruited. Patients were classified into 4 groups (adolescents with NSSI disorder, adolescents with NSSI without impairment/distress, clinical controls without NSSI, and nonclinical controls). Adolescents were compared on self-reported psychopathology and diagnostic cooccurrences. Results indicate that adolescents with NSSI disorder have a higher level of impairment than adolescents with other mental disorders without NSSI. Most common comorbid diagnoses were major depression, social phobia, and PTSD. There was some overlap of adolescents with NSSI disorder and suicidal behaviour and borderline personality disorder, but there were also important differences. Results further suggest that the proposed DSM-5 diagnostic criteria for NSSI are useful and necessary. In conclusion, NSSI is a highly impairing disorder characterized by high comorbidity with various disorders, providing further evidence that NSSI should be a distinct diagnostic entity.

1. Introduction

Given the prevalence of nonsuicidal self-injury (NSSI) [1, 2], its related problems [3, 4], and the findings that it is often present in individuals who are not diagnosed with borderline personality disorder (BPD) [5], NSSI should be considered a distinct diagnostic category. Currently, NSSI is not in the classification system of the fourth edition of the Diagnostic and Statistical Manual of Mental Disorders (DSM-IV) or the International Classification of Diseases, tenth revision (ICD-10) as a distinct entity, but it does exist as a symptom of BPD. So far, several attempts have been undertaken to include an NSSI disorder in the DSM [6, 7], the most recent for the upcoming fifth edition, the DSM-5 [8]. For the DSM-5 NSSI is included as conditions for further study, indicating that criteria sets will need further research before it will be an official diagnosis [9]. The most important justification is clearly the clinical benefit that a distinct diagnosis for NSSI leads to a better understanding, management, and specific treatment. Previously, Muehlenkamp [6] proposed more generally that repetitive NSSI should be established as a diagnostic entity to improve research on this behavior. More recently, Wilkinson and Goodyer [10] proposed in addition to the clinical benefit several positive consequences if NSSI were to be classified as a diagnosis in its own right, such as improving communication between professionals and patients and increasing research into the nature, course, and outcome of NSSI. In addition a diagnosis is also the base to provide financing from health insurances. Currently many patients with NSSI are officially diagnosed with their comorbid diagnoses or with BPD even without fulfilling all required criteria, although, NSSI is their main problem and therefore the main goal of psychotherapy should focus on NSSI. However, without an official diagnosis there is a discrepancy and intransparency between communication to the patient and the health insurance companies. As there is now a definition for NSSI and suggested diagnostic criteria for the DSM-5, it is necessary to test these criteria and to have diagnostic and clinical correlates.

In a recent adolescent community study [11] the prevalence rate of NSSI using the proposed criteria for DSM-5 was 6.7%. However, regarding criterion D it was not assessed whether adolescents self-injured during states of psychosis nor whether they engaged in NSSI when not intoxicated [11]. Data from clinical samples are to our knowledge not available.

One important aspect of a new distinct entity that is also relevant for diagnostic validity is its delimitation in respect to other disorders [12]. Regarding NSSI, a clear differentiation from BPD is needed. Self-injurious behavior is one of nine symptoms of BPD in the DSM-IV-TR. However, although NSSI and BPD can cooccur, they also occur independently. Even early reports warned against subsuming NSSI under a specific personality disorder. Several studies indicated that only about 50% of those who engage in NSSI suffer from BPD [5, 13, 14]. These studies had the limitation that at the time of their investigations, diagnostic criteria for NSSI were not yet available, and thus they used different definitions of NSSI that are not comparable, such as that NSSI has to be engaged in repeatedly (on 5 or more days in the last year). In a retrospective chart review, Selby et al. [15] compared treatment-seeking adult outpatients who engaged in NSSI with a group with BPD as well as a comparison group with various Axis I diagnoses. The NSSI and BPD groups had similar levels of impairment and psychopathology. The NSSI group was characterized by higher depressive symptoms, anxiety, and suicidality than the clinical comparison group. However, most of the NSSI group did not exhibit subthreshold BPD symptoms. As the data were obtained from the charts, no information was available about frequency and motivation for NSSI. Nevertheless, results indicated that NSSI has the potential to be a separate diagnostic entity.

Another important yet difficult distinction has to be made between NSSI and attempted suicide. Three key differences are noteworthy. First, most people engaging in NSSI have, per definition, no intent to die during the self-injuring act. Second, methods and injuries of NSSI are often less severe and usually the damage is not life threatening. Third, NSSI and suicide differ in the frequency of the act, as NSSI often occurs daily [16, 17]. Nevertheless, it is important to highlight that longitudinal studies show that NSSI is a significant predictor for suicidal behavior and most people engaging in NSSI report suicidal ideation [18–20].

The issue of an unclear definition of NSSI also applies for studies investigating methods of NSSI and diagnostic and clinical correlates. Nock et al. [13] and Hintikka et al. [21] investigated diagnostic correlates in adolescents with NSSI. The most common Axis I disorders in adolescents with NSSI were major depressive disorder, conduct disorder, and PTSD [13, 21]. In the study by Nock et al. [13], 67.3% of the sample met criteria for a DSM-IV personality disorder, of which BPD was most common (51.7%). Regarding methods and characteristics of NSSI, Nixon et al. [22] investigated 42 hospitalized adolescents with repetitive NSSI. All endorsed cutting and/or scratching. More than 80% reported almost daily urges to self-injure, and more than 60% reported at least once-a-week acts of self-injury. Seventy-four percent of the adolescents reported having attempted suicide at least once in the past 6 months. Axis II disorders or symptoms of BPD were not assessed in the Nixon et al. [22] study, nor impairment or distress due to NSSI. Clinical correlates indicate that patients with NSSI have difficulties in emotion regulation [23] and, as found in studies of diagnostic correlates, elevated depression as well as externalizing and borderline symptomatology [15, 24, 25].

As yet, there have been precious few empirical studies investigating diagnostic and clinical correlates using the proposed DSM-5 criteria for NSSI and therefore little data support the validity of the criteria. Thus, our aim was threefold: first, to investigate the proposed diagnostic criteria for NSSI for the DSM-5 using a clinical interview with inpatient female adolescents; second, to examine the diagnostic and clinical correlates of adolescents with NSSI disorder; and third, to compare adolescents with NSSI disorder with adolescents with no mental disorders, adolescents with mental disorders without NSSI, and subgroups of adolescents with NSSI such as adolescents with NSSI who did not report impairment or distress. We hypothesized that adolescents with NSSI disorder can be differentiated from other clinical and nonclinical groups. That adolescents with NSSI disorder would be more likely to have a history of suicide attempts, would have more comorbid diagnoses and score higher on self-reported psychopathology, especially borderline symptoms, and would have difficulties in emotion regulation and be more impaired in global functioning compared with the other groups.

2. Method

2.1. Participants

Participants were 110 female adolescents, aged 13–18 years, recruited from different inpatient psychiatric units in Switzerland and Germany. Participants included 41 adolescents who fulfilled the proposed DSM-5 criteria for NSSI disorder, 12 adolescents with NSSI but denied being impaired or distressed due to NSSI, 20 adolescents with a DSM-IV diagnosis other than NSSI, and 37 nonclinical adolescents who had no current or past experience of mental disorder. Adolescents with repetitive NSSI but who denied being impaired or distressed due to NSSI were the only subgroup in the NSSI group that could be used for further analyses. These adolescents indicated in the diagnostic interview repetitive NSSI but denied the questions on impairment and distress in different settings such as family, school, or leisure. In addition they denied questions such as if the patient has to hide the wounds and scars in daily life, if the patient thinks about possible long term consequences of the behavior, and how difficult it would be to stop from one day to the other with NSSI. Demographic and psychosocial characteristics of adolescents with NSSI disorder, adolescents with NSSI without impairment/distress, clinical controls, and nonclinical controls are reported in Table 1. The samples were different with respect to age $F = 6.14$, $p < .01$. Post hoc analysis indicated that this effect was mainly due to the younger age of the nonclinical adolescents group.

Table 1: Demographic and psychosocial characteristics of adolescents with NSSI disorder (NSSI), compared with non-clinical adolescents (NCA), clinical controls without NSSI (CCA), and adolescents with NSSI without impairment/distress (NSSI-C).

2.2. Procedure

All participants and their parents were informed about the study and gave their written consent in accordance with the Declaration of Helsinki. The local ethics committee approved the study.

2.3. Measures: Assessment of Axis I and Axis II Diagnoses

To examine the participants' current or past DSM-IV-TR diagnoses for Axis I disorders, we conducted a structured interview with each adolescent. The Diagnostic Interview for Mental Disorders in Children and Adolescents [45, Kinder-DIPS] assesses the most frequent mental disorders in childhood and adolescence (all anxiety disorders, depression, ADHD, conduct disorder, sleep disorders, and eating disorders) and includes substance use disorders and borderline personality disorder from the adult DIPS [26]. The Kinder-DIPS has good validity and reliability for Axis I disorders (child version, $k = 0.48–0.88$) [27]. NSSI was assessed using the proposed DSM-5 criteria (proposed criteria in 2012). The proposed criteria as of 2012 and the final published version are comparable as follows.

Proposed diagnostic criteria for nonsuicidal self-injury (NSSI) for the fifth edition of the Diagnostic and Statistical Manual of Mental Disorders (DSM-5) (As of November 2012, http://www.dsm5.org/) used for the present study.

(A) In the last year, the individual has, on 5 or more days, engaged in intentional self-inflicted damage to the surface of his or her body, of a sort likely to induce bleeding or bruising or pain (e.g., cutting, burning, stabbing, hitting, and excessive rubbing), for purposes not socially sanctioned (e.g., body piercing, tattooing, etc.), but performed with the expectation that the injury will lead to only minor or moderate physical harm. The behavior is not a common one, such as picking at a scab or nail biting.

(B) The intentional injury is associated with at least 2 of the following

(1) psychological precipitant: interpersonal difficulties or negative feelings or thoughts, such as depression, anxiety, tension, anger, generalized distress, or self-criticism, occurring in the period immediately prior to the self-injurious act,

(2) urge: prior to engaging in the act, a period of preoccupation with the intended behavior that is difficult to resist,

(3) preoccupation: thinking about self-injury occurs frequently, even when it is not acted upon,

(4) contingent response: the activity is engaged in with the expectation that it will relieve an interpersonal difficulty, negative feeling, or cognitive state, or that it will induce a positive feeling state, during the act or shortly afterwards.

(C) The behavior or its consequences cause clinically significant distress or interference in interpersonal, academic, or other important areas of functioning. (This criterion is subject to final approval on the use of criteria that relate symptoms to impairment.)

(D) The behavior does not occur exclusively during states of psychosis, delirium, or intoxication. In individuals with a developmental disorder, the behavior is not part of a pattern of repetitive stereotypies. The behavior cannot be accounted for by another mental or medical disorder (i.e., psychotic disorder, pervasive developmental disorder, mental retardation, Lesch–Nyhan syndrome, stereotyped movement disorder with self-injury, or trichotillomania).

(E) The absence of suicidal intent has either been stated by the patient or can be inferred by repeated engagement in a behavior that the individual knows, or has learnt, is not likely to result in death.

Diagnostic criteria for NSSI according to DSM-5 [9] are as follows:

(A) In the last year, the individual has, on 5 or more days, engaged in intentional self-inflicted damage to the surface of his or her body of a sort likely to induce bleeding, bruising, or pain (e.g., cutting, burning, stabbing, hitting, and excessive rubbing), with the expectation that the injury will lead to only minor or moderate physical harm (i.e., there is no suicidal intent).

Note: The absence of suicidal intent has either been stated by the individual or can be inferred by the individual's repeated engagement in a behavior that the individual knows, or has learned, is not likely to result in death.

(B) The individual engages in the self-injurious behavior with one or more of the following expectations:

(1) to obtain relief from a negative feeling or cognitive state,

(2) to resolve an interpersonal difficulty,

(3) to induce a positive feeling state.

Note: The desired relief or response is experienced during or shortly after the self-injury, and the individual may display patterns of behavior suggesting a dependence on repeatedly engaging in it.

(C) The intentional self-injury is associated with at least one of the following:

(1) interpersonal difficulties or negative feelings or thoughts, such as depression, anxiety, tension, anger, generalized distress, or self-criticism, occurring in the period immediately prior to the self-injurious act,

(2) prior to engaging in the act, a period of preoccupation with the intended behavior that is difficult to control,

(3) thinking about self-injury that occurs frequently, even when it is not acted upon.

(D) The behavior is not socially sanctioned (e.g., body piercing, tattooing, part of a religious or cultural ritual) and is not restricted to picking a scab or nail biting.

(E) The behavior or its consequences cause clinically significant distress or interference in interpersonal, academic, or other important areas of functioning.

(F) The behavior does not occur exclusively during psychotic episodes, delirium, substance intoxication, or substance withdrawal. In individuals with a neurodevelopmental disorder, the behavior is not part of a pattern of repetitive stereotypies. The behavior is not better explained by another mental disorder or medical condition (e.g., psychotic disorder, autism spectrum disorder, intellectual disability, Lesch-Nyhan syndrome, stereotyped movement disorder with self-injury, trichotillomania [hair pulling disorder], and excoriation [skin picking disorder]).

The criteria were reformulated as questions. Interrater reliability estimates for the diagnosis of NSSI were very good ($k=0.90$). Suicide attempts were also assessed at the end of the interview. Master's students in clinical child psychology were first systematically trained in conducting the interviews.

Participants were administered the Structured Clinical Interview for DSM-IV Axis II personality disorders [SCID-II; 29] to assess personality disorders. The SCID-II was found to be suitable for use among adolescents [28].

The Global Assessment of Functioning (GAF) [29] assesses overall patient functioning and symptom severity; these characteristics have been reliably associated with clinical diagnosis, psychopathologic symptoms, and other clinical outcome ratings [30, 31].

The Questionnaire of Thoughts and Feelings (QTF) is a self-report scale (37 items) designed to measure borderline-specific basic assumptions and negative feelings [32]. It is based on cognitive models and Linehan's biosocial model of BPD. The internal consistency within our sample was $= 0.98$.

The Borderline Symptom List (BSL-95) [33] is a self-rating instrument for specific assessment of borderline-typical symptomatology. The symptomatology is collected for the last week. The BSL-95 includes 95 items that are based on DSM-IV criteria, the revised version of the Diagnostic Interview for Borderline Personality Disorder, and the opinions of both clinical experts and borderline patients. It consists of seven subscales assessing self-perception, affect regulation, self-destruction, dysphoria, loneliness, intrusions, and hostility. Within our sample the internal consistency for the subscales ranged from .84 to 0.96. The internal consistency within the present sample for the total score was .98.

The Difficulties in Emotion Regulation Scale (DERS) [34, 35] is a 36-item self-report questionnaire designed to assess multiple aspects of emotion dysregulation. The measure yields a total score and scores on six subscales (nonacceptance of emotional responses, difficulties engaging in goal-directed behavior, impulse control difficulties, lack of emotional awareness, limited access to emotion regulation strategies, and lack of emotional clarity). The internal consistency within the present sample was for the total score, and for the subscales it ranged from = 0.80 to 0.93.

The Functional Assessment of Self-Mutilation (FASM) [36, 37] is a self-report measure of the methods, frequency, and functions of NSSI. The internal consistency within our sample was for the overall scale.

The Youth Self-Report (YSR) [38, 39] measures a broad range of psychopathology. Internal consistency within the present sample was for the total score, for the internalizing score, and for the externalizing score.

The Beck Depression Inventory-II (BDI-II) [40]. The BDI-II consists of 21 items and assesses depressive symptoms in adolescents. The internal consistency within the present sample was .96.

The Depression Anxiety Stress Scale (DASS-21) [41, 42]. The DASS is a reliable and valid self-report questionnaire comprising three scales measuring depression, anxiety, and stress. The internal consistency within the present sample was for the depression scale, 0.85 for the anxiety scale, 0.84 for the stress scale, and 0.94 for the total scale.

2.4. Data Analyses

Logistic regression analyses were conducted to evaluate group differences on diagnoses. Independent variables were the group levels, and the dependent variables the disorders. As we were interested in specific group differences, we set up orthogonal comparisons. The first comparison contrasted the nonclinical adolescent group (NCA) with the clinical groups (CCA, NSSI, NSSI-C). The second comparison contrasted the clinical control adolescents (CCA) with the two NSSI groups (NSSI and NSSI-C, adolescents with or without impairment/distress). The third comparison contrasted the two NSSI groups, that is, the NSSI and NSSI-C groups. Multivariate analyses of variance (MANOVAs) were used to compare the groups (NCA, CCA, NSSI-C, and NSSI) on dependent variables such as internalizing and borderline symptoms, which were arranged based on content-wise criteria. If the Levene test indicated that the variance homogeneity of an outcome was violated, we transformed it for the analysis (log 10 or sqrt). One-way between-groups analyses of variance (ANOVAs) and effect sizes (Cohen's d) were used to assess differences in externalizing psychopathology (YSR external), general psychopathology (YSR total), global functioning (GAF), and difficulties in emotion regulation (DERS). The same orthogonal contrasts as described above were used to analyse group differences. For the comparison of self-injurious behavior between the NSSI groups with and without impairment, two MANOVAs were conducted, for the severity of NSSI (frequencies, and number of methods) and functions of NSSI, respectively. Significance levels were set at .05.

3. Results
3.1. Diagnostic Criteria of NSSI Disorder

The percentages of fulfilled B and C criteria for NSSI and the mean scores of frequency and strength of NSSI symptoms of adolescents with NSSI disorder and of adolescents with NSSI without impairment/distress are presented in Table 2. Data show that for the B criteria, psychological precipitant, frequent urges, and contingent responses were reported by at least 85% of the participants, whereas preoccupation with the behavior and difficulty resisting the urge were reported by less than 50% of the participants. For the C criteria, impairment at leisure time was reported most frequently, and distress was indicated by 69% of the adolescents with NSSI disorder. The highest endorsement (79%) was to the question regarding desire for help, which was added to better operationalize the impairment/distress criteria. This question was also answered affirmatively by 30% of adolescents who denied experiencing impairment or distress due to NSSI.

Table 2: Frequency and percentage of the proposed B and C diagnostic criteria for NSSI for the DSM-5, of adolescents with NSSI (NSSI disorder) and adolescents with NSSI without impairment/distress (NSSI-C).

3.2. Symptoms of NSSI

The frequencies of each methods of self-injury used by the adolescents with NSSI and NSSI-C are presented in Table 3. A group differentiation between minor and moderate/severe methods was not possible, as 94% of the NSSI group and 82% of the NSSI-C group engaged in minor and moderate/severe methods. Table 4 shows the mean number of methods of NSSI performed, the experience of pain, the age of onset of NSSI, and received medical treatment. Further, group differences and effect sizes on severity and functions of NSSI are reported. There was no significant group effect for number of methods used, pain, and age of onset. Moreover, there was no significant group effect for the function of the NSSI behavior, $F(4, 38) = 1.58$, $p = .015$, but the automatic negative reinforcement, $(1, 41) = 4.73$, and positive reinforcement, $(1, 41) = 6.41$, were significantly more endorsed by the NSSI group compared with the NSSI-C group, which is also indicated by large effect sizes (Cohen's $d = 1.08$, 1.21).

Table 3: Frequency of methods of self-injurious behaviour assessed by the FASM in adolescents with NSSI (NSSI disorder) and adolescents with NSSI without impairment/distress (NSSI-C).

Table 4: Means, standard deviations (SDs), and effect sizes (Cohen's d) of the FASM, in adolescents with NSSI (NSSI disorder) and adolescents with NSSI without impairment/distress (NSSI-C).

3.3. Diagnostic Correlates

Axis I and II diagnoses for the clinical samples are reported in Table 5. The mean number of diagnoses was 3.46 (SD = 1.80) for the NSSI group, 1.70 (SD = 1.2) for the CCA group, and 2.09 (SD = 0.70) for the NSSI-C group. According to our data, NSSI was comorbid with other psychopathological disorders in all but two subjects (5%). Major depression was the most frequent comorbidity, followed by social phobia and PTSD. Logistic regression analyses indicated that major depression was significantly more prevalent (OR = 5.78, $p < .05$) among the NSSI group compared with the CCA group. Table 5 shows odds ratios (ORs) and 95% confidence intervals for odds ratios for each diagnosis.

Table 5: Diagnostic correlates of adolescents with clinical diagnoses without NSSI (CCA), adolescents with NSSI without impairment/distress (NSSI-C), and adolescents with NSSI (NSSI), as well as logistic regressions and orthogonal comparisons between clinical controls and NSSI (CCA versus NSSI) and between NSSI disorder and NSSI-C (NSSI versus NSSI-C).

Adolescents with NSSI had relatively more diagnoses of PTSD and suicide attempts compared with the NSSI-C and CCA groups. In our sample, eight adolescents (20.5%) with NSSI fulfilled the criteria for BPD. Adolescents with NSSI but not fulfilling diagnostic criteria for BPD endorsed a mean of 2.3 (, range 0–4) symptoms of BPD. Most frequent symptoms were, other than self-injurious behavior, affective instability and inappropriate, intense anger. Least frequent symptoms were identity disturbances and paranoid ideation/severe dissociative symptoms.

3.4. Clinical Correlates

Table 6 shows results of one-way ANOVAs and MANOVAs. MANOVAs were performed for group comparisons of internalizing psychopathology (BDI-II, DASS subscales, and YSR internal) and symptoms of BPD

(QTF and BSL-95). As expected, the NCA group showed the lowest scores of psychopathology. The NSSI group had significantly higher symptoms of depression (DASS and BDI) compared with the CCA group; there were no significant differences in anxiety symptoms. For the comparison of the QTF and BSL-95 scores, adolescents with BPD were excluded from adolescents with NSSI disorder. Between adolescents with NSSI disorder without BPD (QTF: Mdn = 3.24; BSL-95 : Mdn = 173.34) and adolescents with NSSI disorder and BPD (QTF : Mdn = 3.54; BSL-95: Mdn = 185.06) there was no significant difference, and effect sizes were small regarding the QTF total score ($U = 59.50, p = 39, r = 0.17$) and the BSL-95 total score ($U = 37.00, p = .84, r = 0.05$) but results have to be interpreted with caution as the sample size of adolescents with NSSI and BPD was very small (n = 8).

Table 6: Clinical correlates of non-clinical adolescents (NCA), clinical controls (CCA), adolescents with NSSI without impairment/distress (NSSI-C), and adolescents with NSSI disorder (NSSI), as well as MANOVA and ANOVA with orthogonal contrasts and effect sizes (Cohen's *d*) between non-clinical and clinical groups (NCA versus rest), clinical controls and NSSI (CCA versus NSSI total), and NSSI disorder versus NSSI-C.

The one-way ANOVAs yielded significant group differences for functional impairment (GAF), general psychopathology (YSR), externalizing symptoms (YSR external), and difficulties in emotion regulation (DERS) between nonclinical and clinical groups as well as between clinical controls and adolescents with NSSI. The differences between the NSSI and NSSI-C groups were statistically not significant but showed a trend toward higher psychopathology of the NSSI group.

4. Discussion

We examined the proposed DSM-5 criteria for an NSSI disorder in a female inpatient adolescent sample and investigated diagnostic and clinical correlates of NSSI, comparing adolescents with NSSI disorder, adolescents with NSSI without impairment/distress, adolescents with mental disorders without NSSI, and adolescents with no mental disorders. The results indicated that with the currently proposed DSM-5 criteria for an NSSI disorder, a sample of adolescents could be identified who were more impaired than adolescents who were also hospitalized due to mental disorders but did not engage in NSSI. In addition, 80% of the adolescents with NSSI disorder did not meet criteria for BPD, supporting the evidence for a distinct diagnostic entity.

For the proposed DSM-5 diagnostic criteria for an NSSI disorder, in criteria B (intentional injury is associated with at least two of four symptoms) the highest frequency of agreement was for psychological precipitant, especially sadness and tension, and contingent response, especially relief from negative feelings. The lowest agreement was for preoccupation with the behavior. Results are in line with a community study [11], although they assessed criterion B1 (psychological precipitant) with two items of the FASM and we asked which feelings they experienced just before self-injuring. As in the Zetterqvist et al. [11] study, in our sample there were some ($n = 12$, 29% of adolescents of the NSSI group) who fulfilled the NSSI criteria A, B, D, and E but denied that the behavior caused them any impairment or distress. There is currently a general discussion on whether the impairment/distress criterion should be part of each diagnosis [43] and given the difficulty of objectively operationalizing impairment and distress [44]. Especially for patients with NSSI this might be a difficult question. These patients may see NSSI as a (temporary) solution to reduce distress [10, 11], and so they do not report impairment or distress. In an attempt to better operationalize the impairment/distress criterion, in the structured diagnostic interview Kinder-DIPS [45] there is an additional question: "Do you want help for this problem?" Whereas distress was reported by 69% of adolescents with NSSI disorder, a desire for help was affirmed by 80% and also by 30% of adolescents who denied having impairment or distress due to NSSI. When we compared the NSSI and NSSI-C groups, we found significantly less automatic positive and negative reinforcement as functions of NSSI in the NSSI-C group; furthermore, the NSSI-C group did not fulfil criteria for BPD, had fewer externalizing disorders, and, although not significant, showed a trend of reporting fewer depressive and borderline symptoms and less difficulties in emotion regulation. Future research using larger sample sizes should elaborate on this issue.

The most common methods used for NSSI were cutting, carving, and scraping. This is in accordance with related literature [22, 46, 47]. The method "picked at a wound" should, as also suggested by others [11, 46], be excluded, as this method was also endorsed by 22% of adolescents in the nonclinical group. We were unable to differentiate between adolescents performing minor and moderate/severe NSSI methods due to a huge overlap. In the sample with NSSI disorder, the mean number of types of NSSI performed was 5.42, mean age of onset was 13 years, and 12% had received medical treatment. NSSI is mostly an impulsive behavior that 87% of the adolescents with NSSI disorder reported not thinking about at all or in the few minutes before engaging in NSSI. The most frequently reported functions were positive and negative automatic reinforcement, in line with [11].

As far as we know, this is the first study using clinical structured interviews and the suggested DSM-5 criteria for NSSI to examine diagnostic correlates. Findings suggest that NSSI is comorbid with a wide range of diagnoses. The most common comorbid diagnoses were major depression, PTSD, and social phobia, supporting the results of others [13, 21] and a review by Nitkowski and Petermann [48]. Results are also in line with the chart review of inpatient adults with NSSI [15], characterized by high rates of internalizing disorders like depressive and anxiety disorders. All but one subject had at least one Axis I disorder in the Selby et al. [15] study; similarly, in our sample there were two adolescents with NSSI disorder without any comorbid diagnosis. The comorbidity with externalizing disorders would probably even be higher if the recruitment of this study would not focus on inpatient psychiatric adolescents as in Switzerland female adolescents with externalizing disorders are often placed in residential group homes with outpatient psychiatric and psychotherapeutic services.

Our finding of a prevalence rate of 20% of adolescents with NSSI disorder also fulfilling diagnostic criteria for BPD corresponds to some studies [24, 48, 49] but is lower than the rate of 50% reported by Nock et al. [13]. On the criteria level, adolescents with NSSI disorder without a comorbid BPD endorsed a mean of 2.3 borderline symptoms compared with a mean of 0.3 endorsed by the clinical control adolescents. The least frequently endorsed criteria of the borderline symptoms were identity disturbances and paranoid/dissociative symptoms. Exploring different borderline features might be interesting, as a longitudinal study showed that behavioral impulsivity was an important symptom in explaining frequency of NSSI, low level of affective instability acted as a protective factor, and an unstable sense of self was less helpful in explaining the presence and initiation of NSSI among adolescents [50]. Dimensionally, adolescents with NSSI disorder were not significantly different from adolescents with BPD, although the scores of the adolescents with NSSI without BPD were lower, and for the BSL-95, below the clinical cut-off. Because self-injurious behavior is a criterion of BPD, there can be an association of NSSI and BPD; however, the current results indicate that NSSI disorder can be present without BPD. Nevertheless, future research has to investigate if adolescents with NSSI might develop additional BPD symptoms over time. Other than BPD, no other personality disorders were diagnosed in this sample. There may be a hesitancy to assign personality disorders in this age group [51].

In light of previous studies [11, 13, 21], a somewhat unexpected result was the low rate of alcohol and substance abuse or dependence. There was one adolescent with NSSI disorder fulfilling criteria for present substance abuse. On the interview on NSSI and in the FASM, three adolescents reported sometimes self-injuring under the influence of alcohol or drugs. One explanation of these results might be that the present sample was inpatient adolescents and therefore they did not have the opportunity to use drugs or alcohol on a regular basis. Furthermore, alcohol use in Switzerland is legal starting at age 16 (beer and wine) or 18 (all alcoholic beverages), respectively; that cultural differences might influence the results on an abuse in adolescents. However, as in other studies [11, 13], 54% of the NSSI group endorsed smoking regularly, compared with 10% of the CCA group.

The majority (69%) of adolescents with NSSI disorder reported a suicide attempt, which is in line with the 70% found in the study by Nock et al. [13]. As all adolescents with NSSI disorder endorsed that they conducted NSSI without suicidal intent, NSSI has to be distinguished from suicidal behavior. This is also supported by the reports of some (18%) adolescents with NSSI disorder indicating that they engaged in NSSI to prevent a suicide attempt. Nevertheless, there is considerable overlap between NSSI and suicidal behavior. In two prospective studies, NSSI was shown to be a significant predictor for suicide attempts [18–20]. In our study, adolescents with NSSI disorder reported a mean age at onset of NSSI of 13 years, a mean age of 12 years for suicide ideations, and a mean age for the first suicide attempt of 14 years. This would be in line with Joiner's interpersonal theory of suicide [52] that attempting suicide requires both the desire and the capability to attempt suicide, and NSSI correlates with both. NSSI raises capability by allowing individuals to habituate to self-inflicted pain and violence [13] and it heightens risk for suicidal desire through association with emotional and interpersonal distress [18, 53]. Therefore, it is essential to identify why and how NSSI heightens the risk for suicide attempts.

In addition to the diagnostic correlates, clinical correlates indicated that adolescents with NSSI disorder have, compared with adolescents with mental disorders without NSSI and in line with previous research, elevated rates of internalizing and externalizing symptoms [22, 25], low functioning [15], and difficulties in emotion regulation [23]. These findings complement the picture of highly impaired adolescents with NSSI disorder.

Several limitations of this study should be noted. Our sample consisted of female adolescents admitted to a psychiatric unit and thus may not generalize to other samples. Second, our data were cross-sectional. Third, our subsample sizes were small, so the power was limited for some analyses. Fourth, even though NSSI will be a disorder in Section 3 of the DSM-5 [9], the proposed criteria are not finalized.

Strengths of the study were the use of the proposed DSM-5 diagnostic criteria for NSSI, tackling the problems of previous research on self-injury, where different definitions were used, and investigating samples with repetitive and single episodes of NSSI. Another strength is the use of a multimethod assessment, employing self-report measures and structured clinical interviews.

Implications of these results are that a precise and comprehensive diagnostic assessment including NSSI should be conducted routinely. On one side, NSSI is a highly impairing disorder on its own for the patients themselves, relatives, and friends, and on the other side, it is also a risk factor for suicidal behavior. In summary, our study suggests that the proposed DSM-5 criteria for NSSI are useful and necessary to promote research on aetiology, course, and the development of effective treatment strategies and interventions for adolescents suffering from NSSI.

Conflict of Interests

The authors declare that they have nonfinancial competing interests.

References

1. R. Brunner, P. Parzer, J. Haffner et al., "Prevalence and psychological correlates of occasional and repetitive deliberate self-harm in adolescents," *Archives of Pediatrics and Adolescent Medicine*, vol. 161, no. 7, pp. 641–649, 2007.
2. P. Plener, C. J. Fischer, T. In-Albon et al., "Adolescent non-suicidal self-injury (NSSI) in German-speaking countries: comparing prevalence rates from three community samples," *Social Psychiatry and Psychiatric Epidemiology*, 2013.
3. R. Rauber, S. Hefti, T. In-Albon, and M. Schmid, "How psychologically burden are adolescents with self-injurious behavior?" *Kindheit und Entwicklung*, vol. 21, no. 1, pp. 23–39, 2012.
4. E. Vonderlin, J. Haffner, B. Behrend, R. Brunner, P. Parzer, and F. Resch, "Problems reported by adolescents with self-harming behavior: results of a representative school sample," *Kindheit und Entwicklung*, vol. 20, no. 2, pp. 111–118, 2011.
5. S. Herpertz, "Self-injurious behaviour: psychopathological and nosological characteristics in subtypes of self-injurers," *Acta Psychiatrica Scandinavica*, vol. 91, no. 1, pp. 57–68, 1995.

6. J. J. Muehlenkamp, "Self-injurious behavior as a separate clinical syndrome," *American Journal of Orthopsychiatry*, vol. 75, no. 2, pp. 324–333, 2005.
7. D. Simeon and A. R. Favazza, "Self-injurious behaviors: phenomenology and assessment," in *Trichotillomania*, D. Simeon and E. Hollander, Eds., American Psychiatric Press, Washington, DC, USA, 20011999.
8. D. Shaffer and C. Jacobson, *Proposal to the DSM-V Childhood Disorder and Mood Disorder Work Groups to Include Non-Suicidal Self-Injury (NSSI) as a DSM-V Disorder*, Columbia University, New York State Psychiatric institute, 2009.
9. American Psychiatric Association, *Diagnostic and Statistical Manual of Mental Disorders*, American Psychiatric Association, Arlington, Va, USA, 5th edition, 2013.
10. P. Wilkinson and I. Goodyer, "Non-suicidal self-injury," *European Child and Adolescent Psychiatry*, vol. 20, no. 2, pp. 103–108, 2011.
11. M. Zetterqvist, L. G. Lundh, O. Dahlström, and C. G. Svedin, "Prevalence and Function of Non-Suicidal Self-Injury (NSSI) in a community sample of adolescents, using suggested DSM-5 criteria for a potential NSSI disorder," *Journal of Abnormal Child Psychology*, vol. 41, no. 5, pp. 759–773, 2013.
12. J. P. Feighner, E. Robins, S. B. Guze, R. A. Woodruff Jr., G. Winokur, and R. Munoz, "Diagnostic criteria for use in psychiatric research," *Archives of General Psychiatry*, vol. 26, no. 1, pp. 57–63, 1972.
13. M. K. Nock, T. E. Joiner Jr., K. H. Gordon, E. Lloyd-Richardson, and M. J. Prinstein, "Non-suicidal self-injury among adolescents: diagnostic correlates and relation to suicide attempts," *Psychiatry Research*, vol. 144, no. 1, pp. 65–72, 2006.
14. C. Zlotnick, J. I. Mattia, and M. Zimmerman, "Clinical correlates of self-mutilation in a sample of general psychiatric patients," *Journal of Nervous and Mental Disease*, vol. 187, no. 5, pp. 296–301, 1999.
15. E. A. Selby, T. W. Bender, K. H. Gordon, M. K. Nock, and T. E. Joiner Jr., "Non-suicidal self-injury (NSSI) disorder: a preliminary study," in *Personality Disorders: Theory, Research, and Treatment*, vol. 3, p. 167, 2012.
16. E. D. Klonsky, J. J. Muehlenkamp, S. P. Lewis, and B. Walsh, *Nonsuicidal Self-Injury*, Hogrefe, Göttingen, Germany, 2011.
17. J. J. Muehlenkamp and P. M. Gutierrez, "Risk for suicide attempts among adolescents who engage in non-suicidal self-injury," *Archives of Suicide Research*, vol. 11, no. 1, pp. 69–82, 2007.
18. J. Whitlock, J. Muehlenkamp, J. Eckenrode et al., "Nonsuicidal self-injury as a.gateway to suicide in young adults," *Journal of Adolescent Health*, vol. 52, no. 4, pp. 486–492, 2013.
19. J. R. Asarnow, G. Porta, A. Spirito et al., "Suicide attempts and nonsuicidal self-injury in the treatment of resistant depression in adolescents: findings from the TORDIA study," *Journal of the American Academy of Child and Adolescent Psychiatry*, vol. 50, no. 8, pp. 772–781, 2011.

20. E. D. Klonsky, A. M. May, and C. R. Glenn, "The relationship between nonsuicidal self-injury and attempted suicide: converging evidence from four samples," *Journal of Abnormal Psychology*, vol. 122, no. 1, pp. 231–237, 2012.

21. J. Hintikka, T. Tolmunen, M.-L. Rissanen, K. Honkalampi, J. Kylmä, and E. Laukkanen, "Mental disorders in self-cutting adolescents," *Journal of Adolescent Health*, vol. 44, no. 5, pp. 464–467, 2009.

22. M. K. Nixon, P. F. Cloutier, and S. Aggarwal, "Affect regulation and addictive aspects of repetitive self-injury in hospitalized adolescents," *Journal of the American Academy of Child and Adolescent Psychiatry*, vol. 41, no. 11, pp. 1333–1341, 2002.

23. K. L. Gratz and M. T. Tull, "Borderline personality disorder," in *Distress Tolerance: Theory, Research, and Clinical Applications*, pp. 198–220, 2011.

24. S. E. Crowell, T. P. Beauchaine, R. C. Hsiao et al., "Differentiating adolescent self-injury from adolescent depression: possible implications for borderline personality development," *Journal of Abnormal Child Psychology*, vol. 40, no. 1, pp. 45–57, 2012.

25. J. Csorba, E. Dinya, P. Plener, E. Nagy, and E. Páli, "Clinical diagnoses, characteristics of risk behaviour, differences between suicidal and non-suicidal subgroups of Hungarian adolescent outpatients practising self-injury," *European Child and Adolescent Psychiatry*, vol. 18, no. 5, pp. 309–320, 2009.

26. S. Schneider and J. Margraf, *Diagnostisches Interview Bei Psychischen Störungen*, Springer, Heidelberg, Germany, 3rd edition, 2006.

27. S. Schneider, A. Suppiger, C. Adornetto, and S. Unnewehr, "Handbuch zum Kinder-DIPS," in *Diagnostisches Interview Bei Psychischen Störungen Im Kindes- Und Jugendalter (Kinder-DIPS)*, S. Schneider, S. Unnewehr, and J. Margraf, Eds., pp. 1–62, Springer, Berlin, Germany, 2009.

28. H. Salbach-Andrae, A. Bürger, N. Klinkowski et al., "Diagnostik von persönlichkeitsstörungen im jugendalter nach SKID-II," *Zeitschrift für Kinder- und Jugendpsychiatrie und Psychotherapie*, vol. 36, pp. 117–125, 2008.

29. American Psychiatric Association, *Diagnostic and Statistical Manual of Mental Disorders—Text Revision (DSM-IV-TR)*, Washington, DC, USA, 2000.

30. S. Friis, I. Melle, and S. Opjordsmoen, "Global assessment scale and health-sickness rating scale: problems in comparing the global functioning scores across investigations," *Psychotherapy Research*, vol. 3, pp. 105–114, 1993.

31. R. H. Moos, L. McCoy, and B. S. Moos, "Global assessment of functioning (GAF) ratings: determinants and role as predictors of one-year treatment outcomes," *Journal of Clinical Psychology*, vol. 56, pp. 449–461, 2000.

32. B. Renneberg, C. Schmidt-Rathjens, R. Hippin, M. Backenstrass, and T. Fydrich, "Cognitive characteristics of patients with borderline personality disorder: development and validation of a self-report inventory," *Journal of Behavior Therapy and Experimental Psychiatry*, vol. 36, no. 3, pp. 173–182, 2005.

33. M. Bohus, M. F. Limberger, U. Frank, A. L. Chapman, T. Kühler, and R.-D. Stieglitz, "Psychometric properties of the Borderline Symptom List (BSL)," *Psychopathology*, vol. 40, no. 2, pp. 126–132, 2007.

34. K. L. Gratz and L. Roemer, "Multidimensional assessment of emotion regulation and dysregulation: development, factor structure, and initial validation of the difficulties in emotion regulation scale," *Journal of Psychopathology and Behavioral Assessment*, vol. 26, no. 1, pp. 41–54, 2004.

35. T. Ehring, J. Svaldi, B. Tuschen-Caffier, and M. Berking, "Validierung der Difficulties in Emotion Regulation Scale—deutsche Version (DERS-D)."

36. E. E. Lloyd, M. L. Kelley, and T. Hope, "Self-mutilation in a community sample of adolescents: descriptive characteristics and provisional prevalence rates," in *Proceedings of the Annual Meeting of the Society for Behavioral Medicine*, New Orleans, La, USA, 1997.

37. P. L. Plener, "Functional Assessment of Self-Mutilation (FASM)," dt. Übersetzung. Unveröffentlichtes Manuskript, Universitätsklinikum Ulm.

38. T. M. Achenbach, *Manual for the Youth Self-Report and 1991 Profile*, University of Vermont, Department of Psychology, Burlington, Vt, USA, 1991.

39. M. Döpfner, P. Melchers, J. Fegert, et al., "Deutschsprachige Konsensus-Versionen der Child Behavior Checklist (CBCL 4–18), der Teacher Report Form (TRF) und der Youth Self Report Form (YSR)," in *Kindheit und Entwicklung*, vol. 3, pp. 54–59, 1994.

40. M. Hautzinger, F. Keller, and C. Kühner, *Das Beck Depressionsinventar II. Deutsche Bearbeitung und Handbuch zum BDI II*, Harcourt Test Services, Frankfurt, Germany, 2006.

41. P. F. Lovibond and S. H. Lovibond, "The structure of negative emotional states: comparison of the depression anxiety stress scales (DASS) with the Beck Depression and Anxiety Inventories," *Behaviour Research and Therapy*, vol. 33, no. 3, pp. 335–343, 1995.

42. E. Köppe, *Glückliche Eltern, liebe Kinder: Auswirkun-gen von Partnerschaft und psychischer Symptomatik der Eltern auf das Verhalten ihrer Kinder [Dissertation]*, Technische Universität Braunschweig, 2001.

43. R. M. Rapee, S. M. Bögels, C. M. Van Der Sluis, M. G. Craske, and T. Ollendick, "Annual research review: conceptualizing functional impairment in children and adolescents," *Journal of Child Psychology and Psychiatry and Allied Disciplines*, vol. 53, no. 5, pp. 454–468, 2012.

44. P. L. Plener, J. M. Fegert, and H. J. Freyberger, "Nicht-suizidale Selbstverletzung (NSSV) und Suizidalität in der Adoleszenz," *Zeitschrift Für Psychiatrie, Psychologie Und Psychotherapie*, vol. 60, pp. 27–34, 2012.

45. S. Schneider, S. Unnewehr, and J. Margraf, Kinder-DIPS. *Diagnostisches Interview Bei Psychischen Störungen Im Kindes- Und Jugendalter*, Springer, Berlin, Germany, 2009.

46. E. E. Lloyd-Richardson, N. Perrine, L. Dierker, and M. L. Kelley, "Characteristics and functions of non-suicidal self-injury in a community

sample of adolescents," *Psychological Medicine*, vol. 37, no. 8, pp. 1183–1192, 2007.

47. J. Whitlock, J. Eckenrode, and D. Silverman, "Self-injurious behaviors in a college population," *Pediatrics*, vol. 117, no. 6, pp. 1939–1948, 2006.

48. D. Nitkowski and F. Petermann, "Non-suicidal self-injury and comorbid mental disorders: a review," *Fortschritte der Neurologie Psychiatrie*, vol. 79, no. 1, pp. 9–20, 2011.

49. S. Herpertz, H. Sass, and A. Favazza, "Impulsivity in self-mutilative behavior: psychometric and biological findings," *Journal of Psychiatric Research*, vol. 31, no. 4, pp. 451–465, 1997.

50. J. You, F. Leung, C. M. Lai, and K. Fu, "The associations between non-suicidal self-injury and borderline personality disorder features among Chinese adolescents," *Journal of Personality Disorders*, vol. 26, no. 2, pp. 226–237, 2012.

51. M. Schmid, K. Schmeck, and F. Petermann, "Persönlichkeitsstörungen im Kindes- und Jugendalter?" *Kindheit und Entwicklung*, vol. 17, pp. 190–202, 2008.

52. T. Joiner, *Why People Die by Suicide*, Harvard University Press, Cambridge, Mass, USA, 2005.

53. E. D. Klonsky, T. F. Oltmanns, and E. Turkheimer, "Deliberate self-harm in a nonclinical population: prevalence and psychological correlates," *American Journal of Psychiatry*, vol. 160, no. 8, pp. 1501–1508, 2003.

DOCUMENT 5

The following is a blog post entry by justaquietgirl through the website http://self-injury.net. The post is a sincere representation of the stressors and thinking processes that occur for the self-injurer. Justaquietgirl is describing her pain and confusion throughout childhood with her own eating issues, suicide attempt, and self-injurious behavior. Often in current self-injury literature, the quiet desperation of the self-injurer is described. However, no clinical description can better describe the inner world of the self-injurer than this blog. The blog entry has been unedited purposefully to preserve as much of the originality of the document as possible.

I DON'T KNOW...

By justaquietgirl on February 9, 2014

I've suffered from self harm thoughts for as long as I can remember, I have also had issues eating since I was very young.

I used to watch diet shows, tag along to weight loss clubs with my mum and when I was 8 I stopped eating properly, I used to hold in my stomach and eat next to nothing in school. when I turned 10, I remember standing playing with a knife debating if i would be missed, i also had thoughts of jumping down the stairs. This progressed and a few years back i took a lot of pills and downed some alcohol but it wasn't enough, i shacked a lot for a couple of days though. I lost so much weight last year i fainted a lot and still do. I ended up smoking at a point also which i'm ashamed of. Iused to cut my feet and watch it bleed down the plughole... lately these thoughts have all been coming back and i cut a tinny bit again. I dont trust anyone and i dont know what to do anymore... i need them to go away or im scared it'll get too much.

Source: Used by permission of Gabrielle, www.self-injury.net. Online at https://self-injury.net/blogs/justaquietgirl/2014-02-09-i-dont-know

Glossary

Abuse: Regular and repetitive cruel behavior toward an individual that can be of an emotional, mental, or sexual nature.

Affect: A term that is synonymous with feeling or emotion.

Amygdala: An almond-shaped mass of gray matter that is found in the cerebrum of the brain. A part of the limbic system that is associated with the formation of emotions.

Anorexia nervosa: An emotional disorder characterized by an obsessive need to lose weight through the refusal of food intake.

Anxiety: A feeling of worry or nervousness typically in regard to an impending event or outcome.

Attachment: The process of attaching to an object or person.

Axon: A long string-like structure of a nerve cell that sends impulses from the cell body to other cell bodies.

Binge eating: A form of eating that involves consuming more food than necessary. A term commonly associated with bulimia nervosa.

Body modification: The act of permanently altering the body. This includes tattooing or piercing. Frequently completed for the purpose of adornment, aesthetics, religious beliefs, rites of passage, or self-expression.

Brain: The organizing part of the central nervous system that is contained within the skull of vertebrates. Composed of the cerebrum, cerebellum, brain stem, and spinal cord. Responsible for sensing, organizing, and interpreting input.

Brainstem: A stalk-like portion of the brain that connects the cerebellum and the spinal cord. Associated with the fight-or-flight response.

Bulimia nervosa: A mental disorder characterized by distorted body image and an obsession with losing weight. Involves extreme overeating followed by purging through vomiting, exercise, or fasting.

Central nervous system: A complex of nerve tissue that is responsible for all bodily function. Comprised of the brain and central nervous system.

Cerebellum: Part of the brain found behind and below the cerebrum and above the brain stem. Largely responsible for regulating motor function in the body.

Cerebrum: The most anterior portion of the brain responsible for integration of sensory input, neural coordination, and coordination of voluntary functioning in the body.

Cognitive behavioral therapy: A form of psychotherapy that is characterized by identifying maladaptive thinking and behavior. By changing these maladaptive patterns in thought and action, the individual can experience more facilitative functioning.

Cortisol: A hormone that is released by the adrenal gland when an individual experiences stress.

Counseling: A form of interaction between a trained professional and an individual seeking relief from emotional, cognitive, or behavioral distress in which the two work together to relieve distressing symptoms.

Culture: A set of learned beliefs, values, and customs that is shared by a group of individuals.

Cutting: A term referring to a form of self-harm in which the individual breaks the skin with a sharp object.

Dendrite: The part of a cell body that receives stimulation from a neurotransmitter from the axon of another cell body.

Depression: A state of functioning characterized by sadness, inactivity, and difficulty in thinking and concentration. Often a precursor to major depressive disorder.

Diagnostic and Statistical Manual of Mental Disorders, Fifth Edition (DSM-5): Fifth edition of the American Psychiatric Association publication that provides diagnostic criteria for mental disorders.

Dialectical behavior therapy: A specific form of cognitive behavioral therapy that was developed by psychologist Marsha Linehan specifically for the treatment of borderline personality disorder. It has been used to treat other mental health disorders including nonsuicidal self-injury.

Dissociation: The state of disconnection from emotional and physical experiencing.

Dopamine: A neurotransmitter that is responsible for a variety of brain function including regulating attention and pleasure.

Dysthymia: Persistent mild depression.

Emotion: An affective state of consciousness including, but not limited to, anger, fear, loneliness, pain, joy, confusion, guilt, or shame.

Emotional abuse: A form of abuse characterized by an individual being subjected to behavior that results in psychological trauma.

Emotional dysregulation: Emotional response to a stimulus that does not fit into conventional emotional response.

Empathy: The ability to relate to and understand the experience of another individual.

Epinephrine: A hormone secreted by the adrenal glands as a response to stress.

Excoriation: The process of wearing away the skin.

Fetal alcohol spectrum disorder (FASD): A congenital syndrome caused by excessive consumption of alcohol by a mother during pregnancy resulting in delayed mental and physical development.

Fight or flight: A physiological response formed in reaction to a perceived dangerous event or stimulus.

Frontal lobe: The portion of the brain most closely located to the front of the skull. This portion of the brain is related to personality, learning, and voluntary movement.

Generalized anxiety disorder: A psychological disorder characterized by excessive anxiety about events and aspects of living.

Group counseling: A form of psychotherapy in which a group facilitator meets with a small group of patients to work through personal issues in an interpersonal format.

Hippocampus: A part of the limbic system in the brain that is largely responsible for memory formation.

Limbic system: A portion of the brain that is largely responsible for instinct and mood.

Major self-injury: A form of self-harm that involves the removal of a portion of the body like an appendage or a digit of a finger or toe.

Mindfulness: The process of focusing awareness on the present moment while acknowledging and accepting one's feelings, thoughts, and physical sensations.

Mood: A current state of mind or being.

Neuron: A cell of the nervous system that receives and transmits nerve impulses.

Neurotransmitter: A chemical that is sent from one neuron to another across a synapse. The transmission results in a variety of processes in the body.

Nonsuicidal self-injury (NSSI): Intentional mutilation of the body without the intent to commit suicide.

Occipital lobe: The most posterior lobe of the brain located in the cerebrum associated with vision.

Opioid: (1) A group of natural substances produced by the body in reaction to stress. (2) Synthetic compounds that act similarly to opium.

Parietal lobe: The upper most lobe on each side of the cerebrum responsible for the perception and interpretation of sensation of touch and taste.

Physical abuse: The use of physical force that can result in physical injury. Also see *Abuse*.

Posttraumatic stress disorder (PTSD): A mental health condition that is triggered by a traumatic event either experienced or witnessed.

Prefrontal cortex: Synonymous with the cerebral cortex that covers the front portion of the frontal lobe of the cerebrum.

Psychology: The scientific study of the human mind and its corresponding functions.

Rage: The experience of many emotions at one time resulting in violent outburst.

Rape: Unwanted and unconsented sexual penetration of the vagina, anus, mouth, or other body part of one person by the sex organ, or other objects, of another person.

Selective serotonin reuptake inhibitor (SSRI): A form of medication that is intended to boost concentration of serotonin in the brain. Used to treat depression and synonymous with the term "antidepressant."

Self-concept: The image one has of one's personal qualities such as strengths, weaknesses, and place in the world. Synonymous with self-image.

Self-esteem: The general sense of respect and valuing for oneself.

Self-flagellation: The act of flogging oneself. Often associated with religious practice.

Self-harm: A variety of behaviors including self-injury that involve intentional damage to the body.

Self-injurious behavior: The act of cutting or mutilating parts of the body without the intent of suicide. Synonymous with self-injury, self-mutilation, and nonsuicidal self-injury.

Self-injury: The act of cutting or otherwise damaging parts of the body without the intent of suicide. Synonymous with self-injurious behavior, self-mutilation, and nonsuicidal self-injury.

Self-soothe: The act of providing self-comforting or calming behaviors.

Separation anxiety disorder: A psychological condition characterized by overwhelming anxiety prompted by separation from people with whom a strong emotional attachment has been established.

Serotonin: A neurotransmitter that is related to mood regulation.

Sexual abuse: Any form of nonconsensual sexual contact.

Social anxiety disorder: An anxiety disorder characterized by excessive and unreasonable fear of social situations.

Stereotypic movement disorder: A disorder in which the individual makes repetitive and purposeless movements such as head banging or self-biting.

Substance abuse: Misuse of a mind-altering substance such as alcohol or other drugs.

Substance dependence: A developed addiction to alcohol or other mind-altering substances.

Suicide: The act of intentionally killing oneself.

Temporal lobe: The lobes of the cerebrum located in front of the occipital lobe and behind the frontal lobe. This lobe is associated with hearing and understanding speech.

Thalamus: A part of the midbrain and the limbic system. Responsible for relaying information to the cerebral cortex.

Therapy: Treatment intended to relieve symptoms of a specified disorder.

Trauma: A deeply distressing experience that often results in overwhelming feelings that are expressed through behavior.

Trichotillomania: The compulsive act of pulling out one's hair.

TIMELINE

It is estimated that self-injury has been present for centuries. It is difficult to determine how extensive this practice has been historically as many choose not to share incidences of their self-injury. However, there are important notations in self-injury's historical background. The following timeline represents some of the significant events and dates related to self-injury.

1913   L. E. Emerson coins the term *self-mutilation*. In Freudian terminology, Emerson considered self-injurious behavior a symbolic substitution for masturbation.

1938   Karl Menninger distinguishes self-injury from suicidal behavior in his book, *Man Against Himself.*

1969   In an article entitled, "The Syndrome of Delicate Self-Cutting," Ping-Nie Pao differentiates between delicate (low lethality) and coarse (high lethality) forms of self-injury.

1979   Robert Ross publishes the book *Self-Mutilation.*

1984   Joel Kahan and Mansell Pattison suggest a diagnosis to accompany self-harming behavior referred to as the deliberate self-harm (DSH) syndrome.

1985   The Chronic Self-Destructiveness Scale (CSDS), a measure developed to explore high-risk behaviors typically reflective of impulsivity, is published.

1986   S.A.F.E. Alternatives opens as the first treatment facility dedicated to the treatment of individuals who participate in self-injurious behavior. The facility is considered a world-renowned treatment program.

1987   Dr. Armando Favazza publishes *Bodies under Siege: Self-Mutilation in Culture and Psychiatry,* the first psychiatric book on self-harm. In the book, Favazza also provides the first classification system for the behavior.

1993   Favazza and Rosenthal publish an article entitled, "Diagnostic Issues in Self-Mutilation," in which self-injury was divided into two categories: culturally sanctioned and deviant.

1994   The *Self-Injury Survey,* a four-page self-report measure, is the first instrument developed with the term *self-injury* in the title.

1995   Princess Diana reports on a BBC television interview that she was a self-injurer, providing a new perspective on the behavior.

1998   Karen Conterio and Wendy Lader publish *Bodily Harm: The Breakthrough Healing Program for Self-Injurers.* In this text, Conterio and Lader reveal many therapeutic perspectives and techniques that are used at S.A.F.E. Alternatives, a treatment facility devoted to the recovery of self-injuring clients.

1998   Steven Levenkron publishes a seminal book on self-mutilation called *Cutting.*

1998   The Self-Harm Inventory (SHI), a measure that explores the respondents' history of self-harm, is developed.

2013   The *Diagnostic and Statistical Manual of Mental Disorders,* 5th Edition, is released. Among the changes in this edition of the manual included the first proposed diagnostic criteria for nonsuicidal self-injury.

BIBLIOGRAPHY

About School Psychology. (n.d.) Retrieved February 24, 2015, from http://www.nasponline.org/about_sp/careerfaq.aspx#

American Psychiatric Association. (2000). *Diagnostic and Statistical Manual of Mental Disorders* (4th ed., text revision). Washington, DC: Author.

American Psychiatric Association. (2013). *Diagnostic and Statistical Manual of Mental Disorders* (5th ed.). Arlington, VA: American Psychiatric Publishing.

American School Counselor Association. (2010). *ASCA Ethical Standards.* Alexandria, VA: Author.

American School Counselor Association. (n.d.). *Foundation.* Retrieved February 18, 2015, from http://www.ascanationalmodel.org/foundation

Andover, M. S., & Gibb, B. E. (2010). Nonsuicidal self-injury, attempted suicide, and suicidal intent among psychiatric inpatients. *Psychiatry Research,* 178, 101–105.

Andover, M. S., Primack, J. M., Gibb, B. E., & Pepper, C. M. (2010). An examination of non-suicidal self-injury in men: Do men differ from women in basic NSSI characteristics? *Archives of Suicide Research,* 14, 79–88.

Arhakis, A., Topouzelis, N., Kotsiomiti, E., & Kotsanos, N. (2010). Effective treatment of self-injurious oral trauma in Lesch-Nyhan syndrome: A case report. *Dental Traumatology,* 26(6), 496–500.

Asarnow, J. R., Porta, G., Spirito, A., Emslie, G., Clarke, G., Wagner, K.D., et al. (2011). Suicide attempts and nonsuicidal self-injury in the treatment of resistant depression in adolescents: Findings from the TORDIA study. *Journal of the American Academy of Child and Adolescent Psychiatry,* 50, 772–781.

Badenoch, B. (2008). *Being a Brain-Wise Therapist: A Practical Guide to Interpersonal Neurobiology.* New York: W.W. Norton & Company.

Barrocas, A. L., Hankin, B. L., Young, J. F., & Abela, J. R. Z. (2012). Rates of nonsuicidal self-injury in youth: Age, sex, and behavioral methods in a community sample. *Pediatrics*, doi: 10.1542/peds.2011-2094.

Berg, R. C., Landreth, G. L., & Fall, K. A. (2013). *Group Counseling: Concepts and Procedures* (5th ed). New York: Routledge.

Bloom, C. M., & Holly, S. (2011). Toward new avenues in the treatment of nonsuicidal self-injury. *Journal of Pharmacy Practice*, 24(5), 472–477.

Bloom, J. M., Woodward, E. N., Susmaras, T., & Pantalone, D. W. (2012). Use of dialectical behavior therapy in inpatient treatment of borderline personality disorder: A systematic review. *Psychiatric Services*, 63(9), 881–888. doi: 10.1176/appi.ps.201100311.

Bluth, K., & Blanton, P. W. (2014). Mindfulness and self-compassion: Exploring pathways to adolescent emotional well-being. *Journal of Child and Family Studies*, 23, 1298–1309.

Bowlby, J. (1982). *Attachment.* New York: Basic Books.

Bräunlein, P. J. (2010). Flagellation. In M. Bauman & J. G. Melton (Eds.). *Religions of the World: A Comprehensive Encyclopedia of Beliefs and Practices* (2nd ed., pp. 1120–1122). Santa Barbara, CA: ABC-CLIO.

Brausch, A. M., & Gutierrez, P. M. (2010). Differences in non-suicidal self-injury and suicide attempts in adolescents. *Journal of Youth and Adolescence*, 39, 233–242.

Bryan, C., & Bryan, A. (2014). Nonsuicidal self-injury among a sample of United States military personnel and veterans enrolled in college classes. *Journal of Clinical Psychology*, 70, 874–885.

Cavanagh, J. T., Carson, A. J., Sharpe, M., & Lawrie, S. M. (2003). Psychological autopsy studies of suicide: A systematic review. *Psychological Medicine*, 33, 395–405.

Claes, L., Klonsky, E. D., Muehlenkamp, W., Kuppens, P., & Vandereycken, W. (2010). The affect-regulation function of nonsuicidal self-injury in eating-disordered patients: Which affect states are regulated? *Comprehensive Psychiatry*, 51, 386–392.

Claes, L., Soenens, B., Vansteenkiste, M., & Vandereycken, W. (2012). The scars of the inner critic: Perfectionism and nonsuicidal self-injury in eating disorders. *European Eating Disorders Review*, 20, 196–202.

Clark, J. A., & Henslin, E. (2007). *Inside a Cutter's Mind.* Colorado Springs, CO: NavPress.

Connors, R. (1996). Self-injury in trauma survivors: 1. Functions and meanings. *American Journal of Orthopsychiatry*, 66, 197–206.

Conterio, K., & Lader, W. (1998). *Bodily Harm: The Breakthrough Healing Program for Self-Injurers.* New York: Hyperion.

Corcoran, J., Mewse, A., & Babiker, G. (2007). The role of women's self-injury support groups: A grounded theory. *Journal of Community and Applied Social Psychology*, 17, 35–52.

Crowell, S. E., Beauchaine, T. P., McCauley, E., Smith, C. J., Vasilev, C. A., & Stevens, A. L. (2008). Parent-child interactions, peripheral serotonin, and self-inflicted injury in adolescents. *Journal of Consulting and Clinical Psychology*, 76(1), 15–21.

Davis, D. J. (2014). Mindfulness in higher education: Teaching, learning, and leadership. *The International Journal of Religion and Spirituality in Society*, 4(3), 1–6.

Deliberto, T. L., & Nock, M. K. (2008). An exploratory study of correlates, onset, and offset of non-suicidal self-injury. *Archives of Suicide Research*, 12, 219–231.

Dore, G., Mills, K., Murray, R, Teesson, M., & Farrugia, P. (2012). Post-traumatic stress disorder, depression and suicidality in inpatients with substance use disorders. *Drug & Alcohol Review*, 31(3), 294–302.

Dulit, R. A., Fyer, M. R., Leon, A. C., Brodsky, A. J., & Frances, A. J. (1994). Clinical correlates of self-mutilation in borderline personality disorder. *The American Journal of Psychiatry*, 151, 1305–1311.

Elias, L. J., & Saucier, D. M. (2005). *Neuropsychology: Clinical and Experimental Foundations*. Boston, MA: Pearson.

Elkind, D. (1967). Egocentrism in adolescence. *Child Development*, 38, 1025–1034.

Erikson, E. H., Paul, I. H., Heider, F., & Gardner, R.W. (1959). *Psychological Issues* (Vol. 1). New York, NY: International Universities Press.

Favazza, A. R. (2011). *Bodies under Siege: Self-Mutilation, Nonsuicidal Self-Injury and Body Modification in Culture and Psychiatry* (3rd ed.). Baltimore, MD: Johns Hopkins University Press.

Favazza, A. R., & Conterio, K. (1988). The plight of chronic self-mutilators. *Community Mental Health Journal*, 24(1), 22–30.

Gilman, W. H. (Ed.). (2003). *The Selected Writings of Ralph Waldo Emerson*. New York: Penguin.

Gonzalez, A. H., & Bergstrom, L. (2013). Adolescent nonsuicidal self-injury (NSSI) interventions. *Journal of Child and Adolescent Psychiatric Nursing*, 26, 124–130.

Gratz, K. L. (2003). Risk factors for and functions of deliberate self-harm: An empirical and conceptual review. *Clinical Psychology: Science and Practice*, 10(2), 192–205.

Gratz, K. L., Conrad, S. D., & Roemer, L. (2002). Risk factors for deliberate self-harm among college students. *American Journal of Orthopsychiatry*, 72, 128–140.

Gratz, K. M., Dixon-Gordon, K. L., & Tull, M. T. (2014). Predictors of treatment response to an adjunctive emotion regulation group therapy for deliberate self-harm among women with borderline personality disorder. *Special Series: Selected Papers from the Inaugural Meeting of the North American Society for the Study of Personality Disorders*, 97–107.

Greenspan, S. (1993). *Playground Politics: Understanding the Emotional Life of Your School-Aged Child*. Cambridge, MA: Da Capo Press.

Groot, J. J. M. (2011). *The Religious System of China (Book II): On the Soul and Ancestral Worship*. Nabu Press.

Groschwitz, R. C., & Plener, P. L. (2012). The neurobiology of nonsuicidal self-injury (NSSI): A review. *Suicidology Online*, 3, 24–32.

Grossman, R. (2001). Psychotic self-injurious behaviors: Phenomenology, neurobiology, and treatment. In D. Simeon & E. Hollander (Eds.). *Self-Injurious Behaviors: Assessment and Treatment*. Washington, DC: American Psychiatric Association.

Haberstroh, S., & Moyer, M. (2012). Exploring an online self-injury support group: Perspectives from group members. *The Journal for Specialists in Group Work*, 37(2), 113–132.

Hamza, C. A., Stewart, S. L., & Willoughby, T. (2012). Examining the link between nonsuicidal self-injury and suicidal behavior: A review of the literature and an integrated model. *Clinical Psychology Review*, 32, 482–495.

House, A. S., Van Horn, E., Coppeans, C., & Stepleman, L. M. (2011). Interpersonal trauma and discriminatory events as predictors of suicidal and nonsuicidal self-injury in gay, lesbian, bisexual, and transgendered persons. *Traumatology*, 17(2), 75–85.

Jarvis, G. K., Ferrence, R. G., Whitehead, P. C., & Johnson, F. G. (1982). The ecology of self-injury: A multivariate approach. *Suicide and Life-Threatening Behavior*, 12(2), 90–101.

Joiner, T. (2005). *Why People Die by Suicide*. Cambridge, MA: Harvard University Press.

Juhnke, G. A., Granello, D. H., & Granello, P. F. (2011). *Suicide, Self-Injury, and Violence in the Schools: Assessment, Prevention, and Intervention Strategies*. Hoboken, NJ: Wiley.

Jutengren, G., Kerr, M., & Stattin, H. (2011). Adolescents' deliberate self-harm, interpersonal stress, and the moderating effects of self-regulation: A two-wave longitudinal analysis. *Journal of School Psychology*, 40(2), 249–264.

Kernberg, O. (1985). *Borderline Conditions and Pathological Narcissism*. Northvale, NJ: Aronson.

Kissil, K. (2011). Attachment-based family therapy for adolescent self-injury. *Journal of Family Psychotherapy*, 22, 313–327.

Klonsky, E. D., Oltmanns, T. F., & Turkheimer, E. (2003). Deliberate self-harm in a nonclinical population. Prevalence and psychological correlates. *American Journal of Psychiatry*, 160, 1501–1508.

Lamph, G. (2011). Raising awareness of borderline personality disorder and self-injury. *Nursing Standard*, 26(5), 35–40.

Landreth, G. L. (2012). *Play Therapy: The Art of the Relationship* (3rd ed.). New York: Routledge.

Lau, A. S., Wang, S., Fung, J. J., & Namikoshi, M. (2014). What happens when you "can't read the air?": Cultural fit and aptitude by values interactions on social anxiety. *Journal of Social and Clinical Psychology*, 33(10), 853–866.

Laye-Gindhu, A., & Schonert-Reichl, K. A. (2005). Nonsuicidal self-harm among community adolescents: Understanding the "whats" and "whys" of self-harm. *Journal of Youth and Adolescence*, 34(5), 447–457.

Leahy, R. L. (2003). *Cognitive Therapy Techniques: A Practitioner's Guide*. New York: Guilford Press.

Levenkron, S. (1998). *Cutting: Understanding and Overcoming Self-Mutilation*. New York: W.W. Norton and Company.

Lewis, S. P., Heath, N. L., Michael, N. J., & Duggan, J. M. (2012). Non-suicidal self-injury, youth, and the Internet: What mental health professionals need to know. *Child & Adolescent Psychiatry & Mental Health*, 6(13), http://www.capmh.com/content/6/1/13

Lewis, S. P., Heath, N. L., St. Denis, J., & Noble, R. (2011). The scope of nonsuicidal self-injury on YouTube. *Pediatrics*, 127(3), e552–e557.

Linehan, M. M. (1993). *Cognitive-Behavioral Treatment of Borderline Personality Disorder*. New York: Guilford Press.

Lloyd-Richardson, E. E., Perrine, N., Dierker, L., & Kelley, M. L. (2007). Characteristics and functions of non-suicidal self-injury in a community sample of adolescents. *Psychological Medicine*, 37(8), 1183–1192. doi: 10.1017/S003329170070027X.

Long, M., & Jenkins, M. (2010). Counsellors' perspectives on self-harm and the role of the therapeutic relationship for working with clients who self-harm. *Counselling and Psychotherapy Research*, 10(3), 192–200.

Lovat, P. (2011). Tricyclic antidepressants: Pharmacological profiles. *Nurse Prescribing*, 9(1), 38–41.

Marshall, B. D. L., Galea, S., Wood, E., & Kerr, T. (2013). Longitudinal associations between types of childhood trauma and suicidal behavior among substance users: A cohort study. *American Journal of Public Health*, 103(9), 69–75.

Martin, S., Martin, G., Lequertier, B., Swannell, S., Follent, A., & Choe, F. (2013). Voice movement therapy: Evaluation of a group-based expressive arts therapy for nonsuicidal self-injury in young adults. *Music & Medicine*, 5(1), 31–38.

Matsumoto, T., & Imamura, F. (2008). Self-injury in Japanese junior and senior high-school students: Prevalence and association with substance abuse. *Psychiatry and Clinical Neurosciences*, 62(1), 123–125.

Menninger, K. (1935). A psychoanalytic study of the significance of self-mutilation. *Psychoanalytic Quarterly*, 4, 408–466.

Mohl, B., La Cour, P., & Skandsen, A. (2014). Non-suicidal self-injury and indirect self-harm among Danish high school students. *Scandinavian Journal of Child and Adolescent Psychiatry and Psychology*, 2(1), 11–18.

Moran, H., Pathak, N., & Sharma, N. (2009). The mystery of the well-attended group. A model of Personal Construct Therapy for adolescent self-harm and depression in a community CAMHS service. *Counseling Psychology Quarterly*, 22(4), 347–359.

Muehlenkamp, J., Brausch, A., Quigley, K., & Whitlock, J. (2013). Interpersonal features and functions of nonsuicidal self-injury. *Suicide and Life-Threatening Behavior*, 43(1), 67–80.

Muehlenkamp, J. J., Engel, S. G., Wadeson, A., Crosby, R. D., Wonderlich, S. A., Simonich, H., et al. (2009). Emotional states preceding and following acts of non-suicidal self-injury in bulimia nervosa patients. *Behaviour Research and Therapy*, 47, 83–87.

Muehlenkamp, J. J., Ertelt, T. W., Miller, A. L., & Claes, L. (2011). Borderline personality symptoms differentiate non-suicidal and suicidal self-injury in ethnically diverse adolescent outpatients. *Journal of Child Psychology and Psychiatry*, 52, 148–155.

Muehlenkamp, J. J., & Gutierrez, P. M. (2007). Risk for suicide attempts among adolescents who engage in non-suicidal self-injury. *Archives of Suicide Research*, 11, 69–82.

Nock, M. K. (2008). Actions speak louder than words: An elaborated theoretical model of the social functions of self-injury and other harmful behaviors. *Applied and Preventive Psychology*, 12, 159–168.

Nock, M. K., & Favazza, A. (2009). Non-suicidal self-injury: Definition and classifications. In M.K. Nock (Ed.). *Understanding Nonsuicidal Self-Injury: Origins, Assessment, and Treatment*. Washington, DC: American Psychological Association.

Nock, M. K., & Prinstein, M. J. (2004). A functional approach to the assessment of self-mutilative behavior. *Journal of Consulting and Clinical Psychology*, 72(5), 885–890.

Ouimette, P. C., Brown, P. J., & Najavits, L. M. (1998). Course and treatment of patients with both substance use and posttraumatic stress disorders. *Addictive Behavior*, 23, 785–795.

Pattison, E. M., & Kahan, J. (1983). The deliberate self-harm syndrome. *American Journal of Psychiatry*, 140, 867–872.

Perry, B., Pollard, R., Blakley, T., Baker, W., & Vigilante, D. (1995). Childhood trauma, the neurobiology of adaptation, and 'use-dependent' development of the brain: How 'states' become 'traits.' *Infant Mental Health Journal*, 16(4), 271–291.

Pew Internet & American Life Project. (2010). *Use of Social Media*. Retrieved from http://www.pewinternet.org/

Plener, P. L., Bubalo, N., Fladung, A. K., Ludolph, A. G., & Lulé, D. (2012). Prone to excitement: Adolescent females with non-suicidal self-injury (NSSI) show altered cortical pattern to emotional and NSS-related material. *Psychiatry Research*, 203, 146–152.

Pliszka, S. R. (2006). *Neuroscience for the Mental Health Clinician*. New York: New Age Publishers.

Polster, E., & Polster, M. (1973). *Gestalt Therapy Integrated: Contours of Theory and Practice*. New York: Random House.

Roaldset, J. O., Linaker, O. M., & Bjørkly, S. (2014). Triglycerides as a biological marker of repeated re-hospitalization resulting from deliberate self-harm in acute psychiatry patients: A prospective observational study. *BMC Psychiatry*, 14, 54. doi: 10.1186/1471-244X-14-54.

Rodham, K., & Hawton, K. (2009). Epidemiology and phenomenology of non-suicidal self-injury. In M. Nock (Ed). *Understanding nonsuicidal self-injury: Origins, assessment, and treatment* (pp. 37–62). Washington, DC: American Psychological Association.

Rogers, C. R. (1961). *On becoming a person: A therapist's view of psychotherapy.* Boston, MA: Houghton Mifflin.

Ross, S., & Heath, N. (2002). A study of the frequency of self-mutilation in a community sample of adolescents. *Journal of Youth and Adolescence,* 1, 67–77.

Salter, M., & Breckenridge, J. (2014). Women, trauma and substance abuse: Understanding the experience of female survivors of childhood abuse in alcohol and drug treatment. *International Journal of Social Welfare,* 23(2), 165–173.

Shulman, K. L., Herrmann, N., & Walker, S. E. (2013). Current place of mono-amine oxidase inhibitors in the treatment of depression. *CNS Drugs,* 27, 789–797.

Smith, B. D. (2005). Self-mutilation and pharmacotherapy. *Psychiatry,* 2(10), 28–37.

Smith, N. B., Kouros, C. D., & Meuret, A. E. (2013). The role of trauma symptoms in nonsuicidal self-injury. *Trauma, Violence, and Abuse,* 15(1), 41–56.

Stanley, B., Winchell, R., Molcho, A., Simeon, D., & Stanley, M. (1992). Suicide and the self-harm continuum: Phenomenological and biochemical evidence. *International Review of Psychiatry,* 4, 149–155.

Strong, M. (1999). *A Bright Red Scream.* New York: Penguin.

Sutton, J. (2004). Understanding dissociation and its relationship to self-injury and childhood trauma. *Counseling & Psychotherapy Journal,* 15(3), 24.

Suyemoto, K. L. (1998). The functions of self-mutilation. *Clinical Psychology Review,* 18, 531–554.

Turner, B. J., Austin, S. B., & Chapman, A. L. (2014). Treating nonsuicidal self-injury: A systematic review of psychological and pharmacological interventions. *Canadian Journal of Psychiatry,* 59(11), 576–585.

Van Camp, I., Desmet, M., & Verhaeghe, P. (2011). Gender differences in non-suicidal self-injury. Are they on the verge of leveling off? *2011 2nd International Conference on Behavioral, Cognitive and Psychological Sciences, IPCSIT,* 23.

van der Kolk, B. A. (1989). The compulsion to repeat the trauma. *Psychiatric Clinics of North America,* 12, 389–411.

Vanderlinden, J., & Vandereycken, W. (1997). *Trauma, Dissociation, and Impulse Control in Eating Disorders.* Bristol, PA: Brunner/Mazel.

Vinogradov, S., & Yalom, I. D. (1989). *Concise Guide to Group Psychotherapy.* Washington, DC: American Psychiatric Press, Inc.

Walsh, B.W. (2012). *Treating Self-Injury: A Practical Guide* (2nd ed.). New York: Guilford Press.

Walsh, B., & Rosen, P. (1988). *Self-Mutilation: Theory, Research, and Treatment.* New York: Guilford Press.

Whitlock, J., Muehlenkamp, J., & Eckenrode, J. (2008). Variation in nonsuicidal self-injury: Identification and features of latent classes in a college population of emerging adults. *Journal of Clinical Child and Adolescent Psychology*, 37, 725–735.

Whitlock, J., Muehlenkamp, J., Purington, A., Eckenrode, J., Barreira, P., Baral-Abrams, G., et al. (2011). Non-suicidal self-injury in a college population: General trends and sex differences. *Journal of American College Health*, 59(8), 691–698.

Whittaker, E., & Kowalski, R. M. (2015). Cyberbullying via social media. *Journal of School Violence*, 14(1), 11–29. doi: 10.1080/15388220.2014.949377.

Wilkinson, P., Kelvin, R., Roberts, C., Dubicka, B., & Goodyear, I. (2011). Clinical and psychosocial predictors of suicide attempts and nonsuicidal self-injury in the adolescent depression antidepressants and psychotherapy trial. *The American Journal of Psychiatry*, 168, 495–501.

Yalom, I. D. (1990). Understanding group psychotherapy Video Series, Volume 2, Inpatients. Retrieved from www.psychotherapy.net

Yalom, I. D. (2005). *The Theory and Practice of Group Psychotherapy* (5th ed.). New York: Basic Books.

Young, R., van Beinum, M., Sweeting, H., & West, P. (2007). Young people who self-harm. *British Journal of Psychiatry*, 191, 44–49.

Zlotnick, C., Shea, M. T., Recupero, P., Bidadi, K., Pearlstein, T., & Brown, P. (1997). Trauma, dissociation, impulsivity, and self-mutilation among substance abuse patients. *American Journal of Orthopsychiatry*, 67(4), 650–654.

Zoorob, R. J., Durkin, K. M., Gonzalez, S. J., & Adams, S. (2014). Training nurses and nursing students about prevention, diagnoses, and treatment of fetal alcohol spectrum disorders. *Nurse Education in Practice*, 14(4), 338–344.

INDEX

ABOUT THE AUTHOR

Chris Simpson, PhD, LPC-S, is an associate professor of counseling at Texas A&M University-Commerce. His research interests include the topics of grief and bereavement, as well as nonsuicidal self-injury. Clinically, Chris has worked with a variety of populations in his career including those struggling with chemical dependency, grief and bereavement issues, trauma, and self-injury. In addition to his duties at Texas A&M University-Commerce, Chris maintains a private practice in the Dallas, Texas, area. He lives in Dallas with his wife Kristin.